Opening to Fullness of Spirit

Discovering Secrets of the Soul through Automatic Writing

A Personal Search for Truth

By

Carolyn Greer Daly

2nd Printing-2016

Library of Congress Cataloging-in-Publication Data

Carolyn Greer Daly - 1933 -

Opening to Fullness of Spirit by Carolyn Greer Daly

This book is about an individuals journey into the world of the unknown when asked the question by one of her Sunday school students, "Can you believe in reincarnation and still be a Christian?" In finding the answer, the author is introduced to automatic writing and with this the adventure begins.

1. Automatic Writing 2. Past Lives 3. Metaphysical 4. Spiritual

I. Greer Daly, Carolyn, 1933- II. Metaphysical III. Automatic Writing IV. Title

Library of Congress Catalog Card Number: 2016934578

ISBN: 9781940265346

Cover Art and Layout: www.noir33.com

Book set in: Lucida Fax, PenUltimateLight, Script MT Bold

Book Design: Tab Pillar

Published by:

PO Box 754, Huntsville, AR 72740

800-935-0045 or 479-738-2348; fax 479-738-2448

WWW.OZARKMT.COM

Printed in the United States of America

When the Spirit of Truth Comes

He will guide you into all Truth

For He will Speak whatever He Hears

And He will declare to you

All things that are to come

(John 13:16)

This book is dedicated to the Spirit of Truth and all who open-mindedly make Truth their life's pursuit.

"You Desire Truth in the inward being;
therefore teach me wisdom
in my secret heart"

Psalms 51: 6

The desire for Truth in our inward being is as old as this scripture and as new as the desire of the one who reads these words today.

Endorsements

Carolyn's journey has been quirky and unpredictable. With charm and humor, she describes her unfolding and tentative steps toward welcoming and appreciating her ability to communicate in unusual ways with unusual sources. Like so many with her skills she implies that each of us might open to the possibility of similar experiences. Encouraging. Heartwarming. Entertaining.

Sylvia Ward
Author of the psychic adventure *The Clew*

"What a gifted writer! Carolyn's amazing journey is utterly captivating. Her inspiring story is truly a gift to her readers!"

Patti Intoranat, CHt,
Dolores Cannon's QHHT Recommended Practitioner

"Many of us are being touched by Spirit in ways we could never have imagined. Carolyn's story of her journey between the world we have always known, and the reality that we haven't suspected, is timely and pertinent to the world as it is evolving today. Join her in opening awareness to another realm as she shares her emotional ride into connecting with Truth, and the recognition that unconditional love is the divine answer to everything."

Judy Kerr
Dolores Cannon's QHHT Practitioner

This delightful, loving and entertaining journey into the process of automatic writing illustrates the wide range of experiences possible when connecting to the spiritual realm. As a gifted teacher with over 40 years' experience with automatic writing, the author lovingly shares her own spiritual adventures.

Virginia P. Collier, Ph.D.
Professor Emerita of Bilingual/Multicultural/ESL Education
George Mason University

"Books are written for myriad reasons---to inform, to persuade, and to promote, to expose---but rarely does a book come forth with the sole purpose of sharing. In *Opening to Fullness of Spirit,* Carolyn Greer Daly shares her decades-long journey that began when she dared to question the lessons she'd been taught nearly every Sunday of her life. Her spiritual quest led her to discoveries that alternately astonished, frightened, delighted, intrigued, and comforted her. With honesty and an open heart, she offers this gift of possibilities to you: *Opening to Fullness of Spirit.*

Carol Lallier,
Freelance Editor
(see her website for a list of accomplishments that include, *Goodbye Natalie Goodbye Spendour the story of the mysterious death of Natalie Wood)*

Contents

Acknowledgments

Foreword i

Introduction iii

Chapter 1:

The Journey Begins: April 1972 1

Chapter 2:

Dear John 9

Chapter 3:

Easter Sunday 17

Chapter 4:

Reincarnation: The Story of Ellen 23

Chapter 5:

Threshold of Heaven: Back to April 1972 28

Chapter 6:

Flora Returns: May 1972 38

Chapter 7:

Searching the Scriptures 43

Chapter 8:

The Exorcism of Richard 46

Chapter 9:

Poetry 48

Chapter 10:

Blazing Fires 52

Chapter 11:

Bluebirds Will Lead You: Oval Room Will Tell 60

Chapter 12:

Seagulls Live at the Sea 67

Chapter 13:

Stone House and Bluebirds 73

Chapter 14:
Out of the Closet 76
Chapter 15:
Unity in Charlottesville 79
Chapter 16:
A Course in Miracles and the Coming of the Cosmos 82
Chapter 17:
Pineapples and Opening to the Fullness of Spirit 90
Chapter 18:
Pruning 97
Chapter 19:
The Ghost of Terrace Cottage 105
Chapter 20:
My Mother, the Psychic 115
Chapter 21:
Mother Goes Home 120
Chapter 22:
Springtime in the Rockies 129
Chapter 23:
The Book and Purple Mother 133
Chapter 24:
Seven Young Men of the *Foam* 138
Chapter 25:
Return to Niagara on the Lake, Canada 146
Chapter 26:
Conclusions: April 2002 161
Epilogue: 169
About the Author 175

Acknowledgments

Writing this book has been a spiritual adventure. There have been many dear friends and family members who have shared, inspired, and encouraged me along this incredible journey.

I express my deep gratitude to my good friend Flora May, the only person in my life at that time with whom I could share my secret. Not only did she accept what I was doing without judgment, she became a willing participant in our adventure in search of truth.

My dear friend Mildred, now deceased, was another confidante with whom I could share my daily writing and she could share her writing with me. Her support and contributions to the content of my book were invaluable.

My sister Addy and cousin Judi not only encouraged me to put my spiritual adventures into a book, but insisted.

Thank you to my cousin Carol Lallier and Geege Morgan, my willing Guyenne pigs, who read the first rough draft of my book and gave me confidence to continue.

Most of all I am grateful to my daughter Cindy, who planned trips that took me to places that led to exciting experiences that would not have been possible without her enthusiasm for my spiritual endeavors.

And thank you to Patti Intoranat, my very dear friend who so believed my book worthy of publication that she hand-delivered the manuscript to Ozark Mountain Publishing.

Foreword

I met Carolyn at a mediation workshop and learned of her exploits in automatic writing, which resulted in her communications with entities, souls, in the ethereal universe.

Most of my career I was a physicist. Now, I am an ethereologist, I study the ethereal realm. My specific interests are focused on understanding the notion of BODY, MIND, and SOUL including consciousness of each - independently and combined.

Carolyn's book, *Opening to Fullness of Spirit - Discovering Secrets of the Soul - Through Automatic Writing - A Personal Search for Truth*, takes the reader on her personal adventure to validate and understand God through interactions with entities that passed from this, our material universe. This is important because Carolyn not only describes her communication with souls, but she also takes the steps to ensure that the communication is not from her unconsciousness or some telepathic influence from someone she knows or has met.

From birth to some point in our human experience, society imprints its beliefs, structure, rules, and awareness on us. The point at which our consciousness elevates our personal awareness is different for everyone - for Carolyn it came Easter Sunday of 1971. She did not ask for it, but her soul pushed for her to expand her consciousness. Some would call this a crisis of faith, but for Carolyn it was more - she needed truth and the strength to accept the truth the universe was to give her even though it would crush her social programming.

Interestingly the title of the book provides a great overview of what this exploration is about. It is a journey of 1) *Opening to Fullness of Spirit*, 2) relearning the *Secrets of the Soul*, and 3) *Search for Truth*. All of this to be facilitated by communication 4) *Through Automatic Writing*.

Carolyn's book reaffirms my beliefs in Universal Consciousness - God, exposes me to new truths, and fosters deeper questioning and understanding of my purpose and path in this most wonderful human experience.

As I read through the chapters of this book, I focused on enjoying her adventure. However, as I move from one chapter to the next the breadcrumbs from each past chapters begin to accumulate, and the gestalt, the realization of the Truth, builds and creeps into my mind. Reading Carolyn's book, asking her questions of myself, and evolving and reframing my beliefs is clearly part of this book's journey.

If you choose to evolve your consciousness this book will greatly assist. Don't read it once but several times - truth comes in its own way.

Rex C. Stratton

Ethereal Explorations

Introduction

Should you ever decide to shake your fist at God and demand *Truth*, hold on to your seat and prepare yourself for a spiritual adventure the likes of which you couldn't imagine.

On Easter Sunday of 1971, I did exactly this and found myself propelled across the sea of tradition onto the foreign shores of another realm of reality. In innocent trust I opened a door and stepped over the threshold with no idea where it would lead.

Most stories have a beginning, a middle, and an end. My story is different. I'm not sure when it began, perhaps on Easter Sunday, 1971, or perhaps hundreds of years before that date with a lady named Ellen, and I doubt that it will end with my death. It is my hope that this story will continue when someone else, perhaps a family member, will pick up a pen and find me on the other side.

Chapter 1

The Journey Begins

April 1972

"Bull," I grumbled under my breath. "Some people will say anything to sell a book."

I had just started to read a book entitled *A Search for Truth*, by Ruth Montgomery, and already I was ready to trash it. How dare this woman mislead people with this hokey!

I had come a long way since my Easter experience last year and thought I had opened my mind to just about any possibility, but this was too much. However, it had not been more than a few weeks since I had considered reincarnation nonsense, and now I wasn't so sure. Yes, this book seemed far-fetched, but I had to admit I was intrigued.

It was not too long ago when one of my eighth-grade Sunday School students had come to me and asked, "Mrs. Daly, can you believe in reincarnation and still be a Christian?" I told her that I didn't know. I really didn't know much about reincarnation, except that it was a part of some Eastern religions whose followers believed that after we die our souls come back as cows or butterflies. She looked me straight in the eyes and said, "Mrs. Daly, that isn't reincarnation, that's transmigration. Reincarnation is when you come back as another human being."

"Well," I said, "I guess that proves how little *I* know about the subject."

Then she asked if we could discuss reincarnation in our "free discussion" time at the end of Sunday School class next Sunday.

I had initiated a no-holds-barred free discussion at the end of our class each Sunday for two reasons. First, in my opinion, there was no part of one's life that did not reflect one's belied system. Choices made now, for better or worse, could affect these students for the rest of their lives. I wanted to help them make good choices that would lead each of them to a happy productive life. Second, it helped to maintain discipline during our lesson study time so we could properly cover the required material.

Sometimes these discussion periods sounded more like group therapy than a Sunday School class, and my worst fear had been that one of the students might want to discuss sex. Now I was confronted with one who wanted to discuss reincarnation. Sex would have been easier. Would reincarnation be considered heresy in a Methodist Church? I guessed that it would. However, if we discussed reincarnation and decided it wasn't true, it would serve to reinforce their belief in Christian doctrine. If they were going to discuss it anyway, why not in Sunday School class?

So I said, "Yes," unaware of how much this seemingly casual decision would change my life.

My young student brought me a stack of books on reincarnation on a Thursday, which meant I had to do some quick study before class on Sunday.

I didn't know how much time I would have to spend reading in preparation for our class discussion so I chose the smallest book, *Twenty Cases Which Tend to Prove Reincarnation* by Dr. Ian Stevenson, a professor at the University of Virginia, and it turned out to be a wise choice. His credentials impressed me, and once I began to read I could not put the book down. I stayed up late into the night intrigued by accounts, which, if true, did indeed *tend to prove reincarnation.*

However, this book by Ruth Montgomery was different. Part of it was a "how-to" book on something called *automatic writing.* According to Montgomery, people could just sit down, hold a pen in their hand, and the pen would write all by itself. How could anyone in his or her right mind believe that? Accepting reincarnation was one thing, but accepting this was preposterous. Once more I was about to make a casual decision that would change my life, change my way of thinking, force me to doubt my doubts, and launch me on my own incredible adventure in search of truth. The book I had scorned only a few moments ago as utter nonsense I would soon accept as truth. But this lay ahead.

I turned the page on my desk calendar. It was Tuesday, April 10, 1972.

Okay, I thought, this is most likely rubbish, but I wanted to keep an open mind. I would first follow the instructions to do automatic writing, and after it failed I could condemn Ms. Montgomery for her ridiculous ideas.

I decided that for one week I would devote fifteen minutes every morning following the instructions provided in Ruth Montgomery's book. I would prove to myself the validity, or lack thereof, of Montgomery's wild ideas. However, this did not come without fear. I had always been taught that the fear of God was the beginning of wisdom, and if this was heresy, I did not want to offend God. But at the same time I felt protected, knowing that God knew that in my heart my motives were pure.

My children, Dan, age eighteen in high school; Jim, age thirteen in junior high; and Cindy, age six in first grade, had left for school, and my husband, Tim, left even earlier for work. I was alone in the house and able to sit down in my quiet kitchen and give this automatic writing stuff a try. I approached this quest seriously so I prayed that I would be lead to *truth* as I hummed the old hymn, *"Have Thine Own Way Lord, have thine own way, Thou art the potter, I am the clay, mold me and make me after thy will, while I am humble yielded and still."* When I sat there for ten or fifteen minutes and nothing happened, I wasn't surprised.

I wanted to call my good friend Flora and tell her all about my experiment with something called automatic writing, but I knew she would be leaving for England and Scotland in four days and would be busy packing. On top of that she had friends visiting from New York.

Flora and I had been close friends for several years, and I knew she was one person with whom I could share this information without fear of ridicule. She taught ninth-grade Sunday School at our church, and we had already read and shared ideas on reincarnation and had both come to the conclusion that reincarnation was a distinct possibility.

When on Wednesday and Thursday I went through the same procedure that produced the same results, nothing happened, and I felt I was wasting my time and almost quit.

On the fourth day, Friday, I followed the same procedure. The house was silent except for the rhythmic ticking of the clock as I prayed for *truth* and listened as the words to "Have Thine Own Way" sung softly in my head.

Suddenly there was a strong tug on my pen. I nearly jumped out of my skin, and the hair on my arms stood straight up. I swallowed hard and resisted looking at the paper. The pen gave another strong pull, and I was so frightened I was ready to run. I took a deep breath and prayed for strength to overcome my fear, and as I put the pen back in the writing position the pen began to race across the paper. Finally, I gathered courage enough to look at the paper. There were wavy lines, the letter *"L"* repeated many times followed by a drawing of a small petaled flower similar to a daisy. The marks themselves said nothing, yet their meaning was profound. The writing had *not* come from me! Something completely independent of my conscious mind had made those marks, and I felt the presence of someone or some thing spiritual and terrifying.

Could it be a ghost? And what are ghosts anyway? Are they evil spirits? Do they exist solely to frighten people? I had certainly been gripped with fear when the pen first began to move, but was this movement the fault of the ghost or did the fear originate from within *me*? Are there good ghosts? Are good ghosts called angels? The Bible tells of angels speaking to people many times. If this was true in biblical days, is there any reason why it should not be true today? Had I been contacted by an evil entity, or had an angel sent from God visited me?

Questioning my sanity, I picked up the telephone and dialed Flora's number. Her line was busy.

Damn, this was not the time for her to engage in idle chitchat with goodness knows who about something as mundane as her trip to England when I was standing rubber legged with news that would blow her mind, but I had to wait.

There had to be a rational, scientific explanation for all this. It must have been a muscle spasm, a gigantic prolonged muscle spasm that drew large capital "L's" all over the page and finished by drawing a daisy. Could a muscle spasm do that? I didn't think so.

I needed some fresh air to clear my head so I decided to drop by Flora's and give her a bon voyage gift. I hoped an opportunity to be alone for a few minutes would present itself so I could *try* to explain the bewildering events of the morning.

As I parked my car in front of Flora's house, I saw her dog, Cleo, at her sentry post in the picture window. She stood at attention for a moment, wagged her tail, and spun around to tell Flora I had arrived. I hoped and prayed that Flora would be alone. She was not. To my dismay, her house was full of company, and my head felt like a pressure cooker and the steam was building fast. I really need to talk ... *Now!*

Keeping my lid on was difficult, but I managed to chat casually with Flora and her friends. To my delight Flora's friend had also been reading about reincarnation, and so we had an interesting conversation. However, reincarnation was one thing and automatic writing was quite another. I couldn't share my secret with a stranger.

When I finally maneuvered Flora away from her guests for a few minutes I blurted out in telegram-like sentences my experience with automatic writing. It sounded so zany I didn't expect her to believe me; after all, I could hardly believe it myself.

Before I could finish the story Flora's husband, Mike, her friend, and her friend's husband interrupted us. There was no time for Flora to respond in words to my account of what had happened that morning, but words were not really necessary. Her large blue eyes danced with excitement, reassuring me that I had not lost my mind.

I soon realized that Flora and I would have no time to discuss my experiment with automatic writing today, but I *had* to talk to her before she left for England. I knew I had to wait and waiting wasn't going to be easy.

Flora and I had become such close friends that this was not the first time we found words unnecessary. Our thoughts so often followed the same track that we would simultaneously blurt out identical comments. Our friendship has always been completely honest. Even when we had differing opinions on a subject we did not hold back, and yet the disagreements never provoked anger. We could discuss our deepest religious convictions and yet giggle like schoolgirls at things no one else considered funny. We especially enjoyed teaming up to plan theme parties for our ladies' club. Sometimes the planning was even more fun than the party itself.

Flora's trip to England and Scotland came at the worst possible time. I would miss her. Exploring this new and fascinating phenomenon called automatic writing would be so much more interesting if we could explore it together.

Curiosity and fear had been sparring in my head all day and my curiosity had just scored a TKO. I couldn't wait to try writing again. I must find out the source of this writing and what was causing my pen to move.

I rushed home, ran up the stairs two at a time, landed in my daughter's bedroom, closed the door, and drew the shades. Why I thought someone would be able to see what I was doing through a second-story window in broad daylight, I don't know. Besides, ladies had not been burned at the stake for witchcraft for a hundred years. Was automatic writing witchcraft? If so, what did that make me?

That thought was not intimidating enough to keep me from sitting down with my pen and paper. I began to pray, "Lord, please lead me to truth and understanding, Amen. And PS, Lord, if the truth turns out to be something different than I expect, please give me the willingness to keep an open mind and the courage to accept it."

As instructed, I held the pen loosely in my hand, and with eyes closed and my face turned away, I repeated the words to "The Lord's Prayer."

The pen began to write immediately and this time there were readable letters, all connected as one long word but *I could read it!* The message was clear and I could feel my heart pounding in my chest. Terrified, I dropped the pen and picked up the telephone and dialed Flora's number.

The phone seemed to ring forever before I heard Flora's cheery "Hello."

"I just finished trying to do automatic writing again, and this time I have something I can read," I blurted. "But there is one letter I'm not sure of, and it makes an enormous difference."

I read the message, **"Carolyn, l-o-n-e-l-y here [or l-o-v-e-l-y here]."** It was impossible for me to know if the letter was an "n" or a "v" because the writing bore not the slightest resemblance to my own handwriting. Then it said, **"Just made a note."** It was as if whoever or whatever was communicating with me felt just as surprised as I that communication had begun.

"Who is writing?" Flora asked.

"I haven't a clue," I responded. "It never occurred to me to ask, but I'll try again and call you back. On second thought, I'd better not, I know you are packing for your trip and you have house guests, I won't bother you with phone calls."

"No, no," she said. "Please call, I'm as anxious as you to find out what this is all about."

After I hung up I wasn't so sure I really wanted to know who was writing through me. If the word was "*Lovely*" perhaps it was a visit from an angel sent from God. However, if the letter was an "n" and the word was "*Lonely*," I had to give this *truth* search some serious consideration. If I had been communicating with a ghost who was now living in a "lonely" place, it frightened me. The churches I had attended all my life spoke of Hell as a place of fire and brimstone, but "lonely" seemed even worse. If this were a message from a lonely soul in Hell, the automatic writing would cease immediately.

Suddenly a disturbing thought flashed through my mind. Could this lonely ghost be my mother-in-law? Only eighteen months had passed since my mother-in-law had died. Her name and loneliness had become synonymous. Alzheimer's disease had transformed this lovely lady into a lonely stranger. She had come to live with us when her mind had deteriorated to the point that she could no longer perform the basic essentials of living. Even with my active family around her, she lived in a world apart from us. "God, I do not want this to be my mother-in-law. I'm not prepared for that."

I was shaken by the possibility, but I had asked for it. I had prayed for *the truth* and I had prayed for the courage to handle that *truth, whatever* it turned out to be, I couldn't chicken out now.

I sighed deeply, returned to my daughter's room, and followed my usual procedure, except I spent a considerably long time in prayer.

Almost immediately my pen began to move, and I noticed for the first time a tingling sensation in my right hand. My heart pounded as an image of the tortured face of my mother-in-law flashed before my eyes.

Suddenly I felt a reassuring *Presence* and my fears evaporated, tears filled my eyes, and at that moment I felt closer to God than I had ever felt before and I knew *the truth of His being, for there before me were written these words:* ***"Do not be afraid my child, I am with you always, Jesus."***

Chapter 2

Dear John

My feeling of awe and wonder was suddenly interrupted when the front door swung open and in bounced Cindy, all bubbles and sunshine, spouting excitedly of her upcoming first-grade class trip to the Washington, D.C., Zoo on April 18. Naturally, she had volunteered me to accompany her class, and I tried to be delighted. Through the years I had always enjoyed going on field trips with my children's class, yet this time it meant I couldn't write. I had only written two sentences, and already I wondered if automatic writing could become an obsession. Somewhere deep inside I knew that it could, but at this moment it didn't matter. I didn't have time to deal with that possibility now. As Cindy made a mad dash for the bathroom, I made a mad dash into her room, snatching up my papers and stuffing them into the nearest drawer.

Cindy continued to chatter excitedly about her zoo trip, but her words flew over my head. How could I think of an upcoming zoo trip when I was caught up in a whirlwind of exhilaration, joy, and deep humility? I wanted to shout my amazing new secret for all to hear so that everyone might experience the feeling of grace that was mine today. For the moment, however, I must contain myself, at least until I learned more about what I was doing. I didn't want to be known as "that crazy old lady of Lanham who communicates with ghosts."

I was relieved when Cindy went out to play. I seized the opportunity to return to her room, lock the door, and grab my paper and pen from the drawer. As soon as I put pen to paper, my hand began to move. I rallied my courage, and this time I watched.

Slowly and carefully letters were shaped on the paper in handwriting entirely different from my own. As the letters were taking shape, I had no idea what letter was being formed or what was coming next. My first message was repeated, but this time it was written more clearly: **"LoVely here."** I heaved a great sigh of relief!

I astonished myself when I spoke aloud to the spirit guiding my hand. "Who are you? Please identify yourself." This time I sensed somehow the message was not from Jesus. Again, I whispered to the unseen entity, "Please, identify yourself. Who is with me now? Who or what is causing my pen to write?" Again the pen began to move slowly and deliberately forming a capital **L** then **o v e r**. **"Lover?"** "What the dickens is this?" I whispered to the empty room. "Who are you?"

Once again the pen began to form letters. This time the letters were different. **"J.o.h.n."**

"John?" I puzzled. "John is a very common name; surely I must have known someone in my life that is now on the other side by the name of John." I drew a blank. Then it hit me. If Jesus had written a few hours earlier, this must be John the Baptist. The thought was interrupted by another hard tug on the pen. **"Lover, Lover,"** it wrote, dashing merrily across the page, **"Carolyn and John are Lovers."** My pen and my chin dropped at the same time. "Well," I thought, "that pretty well eliminates John the Baptist."

I had to find out more about this character who called himself John, but one glance at the clock told me that Tim would be coming home in about five minutes and I had to hide these papers. I could only imagine the problems it would cause if Tim were to read what was written on the paper. He would think I had a lover named John. And imagine my explanation, the truth. I would either be served with divorce papers, or he would have me committed to a mental institution. I didn't like my options. I would have to hide this little secret from Tim, at least for now.

In near panic, I stuffed the papers in an old handbag and pushed it far back on the closet shelf.

I ran to the kitchen and pulled out a package of hotdogs from the freezer. Tim hates hotdogs, but I didn't have time to care. Tim is always ready to eat within three to five minutes after entering the front door, so I used a little trick to lull him into thinking dinner was almost ready. I quickly set the table. This gave me time to throw dinner together.

For the rest of the evening I felt like an incompetent actress playing the part of a normal, dutiful, loving housewife, making silly jokes and small talk, all the while my mind was secretly on "Lover John."

I was desperate to call Flora. She was the only person with whom I could discuss my strange experience, but time was running out. My family would be close to home all weekend, and Flora was leaving for England on Sunday. Here I was, having the most incredible experience of my life and there was no one with whom to share it.

I was eager to find out more about this spooky lover, but where could I go to have the necessary privacy? The bathroom. I removed the wrinkled papers from the old purse, stuffed them in my pocket, proceeded to the bathroom, and locked the door. Sitting on the toilet seat, with my paper on the countertop, I began to pray.

As soon as my pen touched the paper, the pen began to move. The message was fascinating, and I became totally engrossed and completely lost track of time until there was a knock on the bathroom door. I screamed. My scream startled my husband, and he responded with a little scream of his own.

"Damn it, Carolyn, I only wanted to know if you were okay. You've been in the bathroom a long time and I thought you might be sick."

"I was just fine until you frightened me to death," I said in a saccharine-coated voice.

I flushed the toilet purely for sound effects and gave up, at least temporarily, any further attempt to communicate with John tonight but oh how I resented it. My robot body returned to be with the family; my mind did not.

With the family gathered around the television set for the rest of the evening, another attempt at writing seemed impossible. I tried very hard to concentrate on the television program and the chitchat of the family, but I couldn't.

I picked up a scrap of paper and a pencil and even without a prayer the pencil began to write. *"Lover John."* I quickly wadded the scrap of paper in a tight fist. The nerve of that spook to write those words when my husband is sitting not more than six feet away.

Cindy's curiosity must have been aroused because she peered over my shoulder and asked, "What are you drawing, Mommy?"

"Just doodling, honey," I lied.

I looked at my family sitting there completely engrossed in a fictional television drama. I wondered what their reaction would be if I were to tell them about the events taking place for the past several days right under their noses. A week ago I also would have been engrossed in the television drama but not tonight. Compared to my true experiences, television was a bore. Compared to my true experiences of the past week, anything fictional was a bore!

I was antsy to write and frustrated that I couldn't. If only the family would go to bed early it would allow me to sneak in a writing session. But it didn't happen. It was after midnight when they finally decided to go to bed. In order not to raise suspicion, I also went to bed and waited until I was sure Tim was asleep.

At last my time had come. I slithered silently out of bed so as not to awaken Tim and crept into the kitchen not daring to even turn on the light. It was almost 2:00 a.m.

In the quiet darkness, my home seemed haunted by an intangible presence. I was frightened, but I was also curious. "Who is this *'lover John'*?" My skin was clammy, and I could hear my pulse throbbing in my ears. Just as I put my pen to paper something soft brushed against my leg. My mouth opened in a silent scream, and I saw two large green eyes glowing in the darkness. I heaved a sigh of relief as I realized it was only my cat, Oscar, rubbing against my legs. This time it was fear that scored the TKO over curiosity, and I was certain I could never do automatic writing at night. I was wrong.

I tiptoed hurriedly down the hall and into bed and snuggled as close to Tim as I could possibly get. Even though it was a comfort to be close to my real-life husband, my eyes would not close and my mind would not shut up. For hours I lay there and listened as the house made moaning noises I had never noticed before as I relived and tried to evaluate the events of the past few days. I whispered an apology to Ruth Montgomery and vowed to finish her book as soon as possible.

Saturday, April 15, 1972

As dawn finally arrived the anxieties of the night before departed. Even though I had slept very little during the night, I welcomed the new day with enthusiasm, excitement, and about thirty or forty sneezes. Since about the age of thirteen or fourteen I had awakened each morning sneezing. I had no idea what I might be allergic to, but it was so normal for me that I hardly noticed it. However, this morning was special; I couldn't wait to see what surprises the new day would bring. Were the weird dreamlike events of the past few days utter fantasies or was there a rational scientific explanation? Could it have been my own hand that had made the pen move? Or might it have been *my* subconscious mind? What was the subconscious mind anyway? No two "experts" seemed to be able to agree on a definition. Could the message from Jesus have been an attempt of my subconscious to make a demigod of myself? Was "Lover John" a manifestation of a subconscious desire to have a romantic interlude that my rational conscious mind would find unacceptable? I knew I had to find the answer within myself; someone else's opinion wouldn't do. After all, opinion is only someone else's interpretation of what they think they know.

I couldn't have imagined at that point in time that the fascinating adventure into my psyche would last a lifetime and would bring so many exciting surprises. I had just taken my first steps along a path of spiritual adventure and had no idea where it would lead.

At this moment I only knew that I had to write again, and soon. How do I get rid of the family? At last Dan, Jim, and Cindy went outdoors, and Tim decided to take advantage of the warm spring weather to wash the car.

The moment the door closed behind him I was seated in Cindy's room with the door locked, the shades drawn, and ready to write. I had planned to spend more time in prayer, but as soon as the pen touched the paper it began to move. The words **"Lovely here, lovely here, John calls, John and Carolyn are lovers. ... come, come, Lovely here."** were repeated many times. I was puzzled. Was this "Lover John" a ghost who wants me to die and join him in his "Lovely" world of spirit? That was scary! I needed to talk to someone, and I knew it couldn't be Tim, at least not now. The words on the paper embarrassed me. It was not the beautiful spiritual messages that Ruth Montgomery had received. Why? The words from *Lover John* gave me an uneasy feeling, especially the invitation to "come." That hinted of my death.

I dialed Flora's number and without even "hello, how are you," I whispered, "I'm writing again and you won't believe what it's telling me. There is this character named John, who claims to be my lover." I chuckled.

Flora's voice was too controlled and matter of fact. I knew she was not alone. As I read to her everything that had been written the last few days, I held my pen loosely in my hand, placed it on the calendar pad, and the pen began to write. Even as I was talking, words began to form right before my eyes, and I couldn't believe what I was seeing. "Flora," I whispered, "the pen is writing at this very moment."

Flora gasped, "The hair on my arms is standing on end; tell me what it's writing."

On my calendar pad in the smallest writing I have ever seen and without a break between words, the pen wrote, **"Lover I come, I call, Carolyn can write."**

"Do you believe this, Flora?" I asked.

"Yes," she said in a hushed voice, "tell me more." There was no doubt that she was interested, but there was also no doubt that she was not alone.

The power in my hand became stronger, and the writing became more legible. When I looked at the words I was shocked.

It said, **"Easter, Carolyn called on Jesus, Easter, Easter, Carolyn called Jesus ... Cold, cold, John."** I was dumfounded not only by the strange words, but also by the cold, numb feeling in my writing hand. I lifted both my hands and gently touched my cheeks. There, to my horror, was a pronounced difference. My left hand, that had been perfectly still, holding the phone, was as warm as normal, but my right hand, through which John had been writing, was as cold as a corpse.

My voice trembled as I resumed the conversation and told Flora what had just happened. "Why is my writing hand so cold, and how does John know about my horrible experience of Easter Sunday almost a year ago?"

Flora put into words exactly what I was thinking. "Could Easter Sunday last year have been the real beginning of what is happening now?"

Our conversation ended abruptly when Tim stuck his head in the door and asked me to bring him the Windex. Flora asked me to keep her posted on any new developments, and I promised that I would. After I took the paper towels and window cleaner to Tim, I picked up the papers and tore off the calendar page to study them further. For the first time since I had started to write I thought it would be a good idea to put a date and time at the top of the page. My papers were accumulating, and I needed to know which came first. As I began to study them and try to make sense of them, Tim called me again to fetch something else. I found the interruptions annoying and my disposition deteriorating. As I again hid the papers in the old purse, I gave myself a good dressing down. It wasn't fair to the family to exclude them from my thoughts and become annoyed when they interrupted them. I'd better get back to the world of the living. I vowed there would be no more automatic writing until the family was completely away from the house. I vowed to stop thinking about the writing and its possible connection to that awful Easter Sunday in 1971.

It was a well-intended vow, but it was broken almost immediately. The more I tried not to think of last Easter Sunday, the more the memory haunted me.

If only Flora were not leaving the next evening for England; if only John had chosen a better time to make himself known to me; if only I had nerve enough to tell Tim the whole story. I tried to join the activities of the family. My body was there, but my mind was in another world.

Is automatic writing becoming an obsession? Is it taking over my life? No, no, I wouldn't allow that. I was much too strong to allow anything to spoil my family life; at least, that is what I hoped.

I also decided to ask in prayer for a cleansing of my soul, in the way Jesus had cleansed the temple. I didn't know what was there that didn't belong so I asked that all negative, self-destructive thinking known to me and unknown to me be purged from my soul. The next time the house was empty and quiet, I would meditate and ask for the Lord to cleanse my temple. However, this was a busy weekend, and for the moment my meditative prayer had to be postponed.

The nagging memory of last Easter continued to haunt me and as much as I tried to fight it, I lost the battle. I knew I must analyze the events of last Easter in the light of the discoveries of the last few days.

I told the family I needed a nap and slipped into my bedroom, closed the door, closed my eyes, and relived Easter Sunday, 1971.

Chapter 3

Easter Sunday

Yes, I thought, Easter Sunday in 1971 was the real beginning, and I could remember every ugly detail as if it were happening all over again.

At the time I was teaching an eighth-grade Sunday School class in Lanham, Maryland, and thought I knew all there was to know about God, Jesus, and the Holy Spirit. After all, I was raised in the Baptist Church, and there could be no *truth* other than the one I had been born into, all else was heresy. That's what I was taught and that was what I *tried* to believe. I had taken a major step by moving my membership from the Baptist Church to the Methodist Church without feeling like a heretic. Then came my dark night of my soul.

Why on Easter Sunday did I suddenly feel something was wrong, something was missing, when my external life was so good? The struggle of helping to put Tim through college was over. Tim was earning more money than we'd ever had in our lives. We had three wonderful children and had recently moved into a lovely new home. I'd come a long way from the one-bedroom apartment on D Street, N.E. in Washington, D.C. My American dream had come true.

It should have been like every other Easter Sunday morning. The children come into our bedroom to awaken us, we go downstairs to hunt for Easter eggs, dress in our Sunday best, and go to Easter Sunday service. But this Easter was different, terribly different. I didn't want to open my eyes; I didn't want to speak to anyone; and I didn't want anyone to speak to me. I felt as if a hate bomb had exploded in my head. I glanced at Tim sleeping peacefully beside me as the thundering voice of rage screamed in my head. Tim had no right to sleep in this morning. *I* had been the one to stay up late, hiding Easter eggs and putting the finishing touches on the outfit that I had made for little Cindy. My exploding brain told me to pull Tim out of bed by the hair of his head, but I resisted.

It was only with the utmost effort that I dragged myself into the bathroom, splashed water onto my face, and glanced into the mirror. The reflection glaring back at me sent shivers down my spine. I looked like Snow White's wicked stepmother. Could this be me or had an evil demon invaded my body?

With every ounce of mental energy I could muster, I fought to control the raging hate within me. How could I let my children down on Easter morning? There were big plans today. As soon as the children found their eggs and candy we would leave for church. I would accompany my eighth-grade Sunday School class to Easter services in the sanctuary, and after church our relatives would be coming over for a big Easter dinner.

Part of me didn't want to disappoint anyone but that evil other part didn't give a damn. I hated everyone. Most of all I hated myself, and that hate was reflected in my hideous face. As I fought to control the demonic intruder, I began to question my sanity. This was a day like no other. Just at the time my life seemed perfect, I was experiencing the ugliest day of my life. My soul was under attack, and I was afraid I was losing the battle.

With dread and self-pity I thought of the things *I had* to do: *I had* to be kind to my husband and children, *I had* to help the children dress, *I had* to start the ham before I left for church, *I had* to drive the children to church, and *I had* to accompany my eighth graders to Easter services. I fought with myself to remain civil with my family. I put on the coffee, watched the children find their Easter goodies, and felt relieved to see Tim go out the door on his way to the bakery to buy fresh rolls for breakfast. At least for the moment he was safely out of range of my rage. Everything I picked up I wanted to throw; every time I opened my mouth I wanted to scream.

I yanked a dress from its hanger and threw it on the bed. Although it was not brand new, on another day I would have found it attractive. Today it was an ugly rag hanging on an ugly witch. I wanted to rip it to shreds, but once more I resisted.

No sooner had Dan, Jim, and Cindy piled into the car than they began to bicker. All wanted to ride in the front seat with me. Again, I resisted a scream. In a very controlled voice I whispered, "Please, let's not have any squabbling today, it's

Easter Sunday, it's a beautiful morning, don't spoil it. Besides, I have a miserable headache."

As we approached the church I saw familiar faces of people who had been my friends for twelve or thirteen years, but today I looked at them with complete contempt. *Hypocrites! Easter Christians!* Today you come to church, and for many of you it is the only Sunday in the year you attend church and some of you are coming only to show off your new Easter outfits!

From the corner of my eye I caught a glimpse of the back of a friend approaching the church with her family. Her obviously expensive dress barely covered her fat behind, and the flesh on her pudgy legs bounced as she walked. Before today I had liked her, found her witty and friendly, but today I could only recall the many times I had seen her at a dance or a party when she had too much to drink. Today she was a hypocrite joining the other hypocrites who would raise their voices in song, *"Up from the grave He arose, a mighty triumph o'er His foes, He arose, He arose, Hallelujah Christ arose."*

How many of the people singing this song today actually believed the words coming from their lips? How many ministers preaching the resurrection message actually believed it?

Like a thunderbolt it hit me. *I was the one who didn't believe. I was the hypocrite!* Deliberately, I had refrained from purchasing a new Easter outfit. From this I was supposed to gather some smug self-righteous esteem. It hadn't worked.

As an eighth-grade Sunday School teacher, I was expected to participate in the celebration of the resurrection of Jesus. Today I didn't believe in the resurrection. Today I wasn't even sure I believed in Jesus.

There was no way I could take my class to Easter worship service. I spotted my good friend Mildred Morrow, who taught seventh-grade Sunday School, and asked her to accompany my class to church. I told her I had a splitting headache. I was sure Mildred would be the only person entering the church for the right reason. Mildred was no hypocrite. The headache was real, but it was not the reason I left my class and children to race home.

Tim was shocked to see me bolt through the front door and slam it behind me. He was in the midst of his usual Sunday morning routine: reading the newspaper, eating warm bakery rolls dripping with melting butter, and sipping his coffee. "I thought you and the kids were going to church," he said. "Is anything wrong?" He was obviously puzzled.

"Yes!" I said, as the suppressed anger exploded into sobs. I tried to explain to Tim my horrible mood, the feeling that everything I thought I had believed all my life was based on a lie, that all Christian churches were perpetuating that lie to fill pews and collection plates. They preached and condemned other religions from the pulpit and said only those who believe in the virgin birth, death, and resurrection of Jesus would be allowed in heaven and the rest of the world would go to Hell. Worst of all I doubted that most of those who were preaching these sermons actually believe it themselves. How could any reasonable, open-minded person believe that the religion they were so fortunately born into was the only one with the *truth*? I was overcome with the recognition of my own hypocrisy that I now realized was the underlying cause of my agony.

It was a rather strange scene. Here I was, a Sunday School teacher of more than five years, confessing to a husband who never attended church, all my doubts in the faith I taught. I told Tim how much I loved my students, but I knew I could not continue to teach something in which I did not believe and Tim agreed. Giving up my eighth graders whom I loved so much broke my heart, but I felt at that moment it was something I had to do.

I asked Tim if he believed in the resurrection sermons being delivered all over the Christian world today. Ironically, his reply was "yes."

Tim helped me prepare the ham for the oven and put the house in order before our relatives arrived and even volunteered to pick up the children from church. Some of the pressure was released, but the underlying doubts continued to torture me.

As soon as Tim left to fetch the children, I went into the bedroom, slammed the door, and fell to my knees. The one thing I did not doubt was the existence of God, and I felt sure that somewhere within the reach of humankind was the *Truth* about God. It was for this *Truth* I prayed. "*Prayed*" was not quite the right word. I arched my neck, shook my fist, and in a sobbing rage, demanded, *"God, Jesus, or whatever you call yourself, you know who you are, I WANT TRUTH!"* Confronting my doubts, fears, and feelings relieved some of the pressure. As I started to leave the room, I decided there should be a P.S., *"God, or whoever you are, if the Truth turns out to be something I don't want to accept, please give me the courage to accept it ... even if it's Catholic!"* For a girl brought up in a fundamentalist Baptist Church, this possibility posed the ultimate challenge. Non-Christian beliefs didn't even enter my thoughts. For the first time in my life I cried out for *truth* because for the first time in my life I was not sure that I already knew it.

It was with a more solemn attitude I prayed for strength to perform the tasks that lay before me this day with a cheerful demeanor that would not betray the vicious monster that was still tormenting me. When I finished the prayer and left my bedroom, I felt a little better, but I knew this was just the beginning and I had much to deal with in the days to come. Boy, was I right!

At about dusk our guests left. I immediately went to my room, locked the door, fell on my bed, and allowed the pent-up sobs to flow. *"Jesus, Jesus,"* I cried, *"if you are Truth, or if any Christian church is the real Truth, I want to know which one it is."* Thoughts flooded my mind faster than I could comprehend them. The pope has studied religion most of his life, he was born a Catholic, and he remains a Catholic; our local rabbi has studied religion most of his life, he was born a Jew and remains a Jew; our minister has studied religion most of his life, he was born a Methodist and remains a Methodist. And, in spite of the many Christian missionaries sent to "save" them, even Buddhists, Hindus, and Muslims have for the most part remained in the religion into which they were born. *"Who is right? Which religion is closest to pure Truth? Was I so fortunate as to be born into the only True religion? Am I a Christian because I was lucky enough to be born to a Christian family, or am I a Christian because that is what I truly believe?"* That was one question I knew I had to answer in order to find peace of mind and so began my lifelong quest. I didn't know much about other religions, but I knew the time had come to find out.

..ought it was a little like being born into a family of Democrats or Republicans and staying with that party only because it had been the choice of your family for generations. It was allowing someone else to do your thinking for you, and I was now ready to do my own thinking and come to my own conclusions.

The subject was too complex for my exhausted mind to struggle with on this night. I would think about it tomorrow when my mind was fresh and perhaps the demon would go away and bother someone else.

I opened the door a crack and told the family that I had a headache and was going to bed early. I changed into my pajamas and fell into bed mentally and physically exhausted yet I could not relax. At some point I was vaguely aware of Tim coming to bed. I resented his presence and moved as far away from him as possible. Obviously, traces of the hate bomb lingered still, and my sleep was fitful.

Much later in the night my sleep was interrupted by something that felt like an electrical shock, short-circuiting every muscle in my body. I jolted with such force that I awakened Tim. He put his arms around me and asked if I'd had a bad dream. "No, hon," I replied, "everything is just fine." And it was. The evil intruder had left me, and I was my old self again. For the first time in nearly twenty-four hours I had been able to feel love. This, I thought, must be the difference between heaven and hell. Heaven is being able to love and hell is when you can't. It was good to be back in heaven.

Now, a year later I would remember this day in great detail, ponder its meaning, and recognize that this day had been the turning point of my spiritual life and the beginning of a wondrous adventure. John must have known this and reminded me by writing, **"Easter, Easter, Carolyn called on Jesus."** Could it be that automatic writing was a partial answer to my prayer on that Easter Sunday?

Chapter 4

Reincarnation

The Story of Ellen

I wanted desperately to share my experience with others but who would that be? Tim's practical, down-to-earth, intelligent reasoning mind steered clear of conversations regarding religion. Besides, how could I explain "Lover John?" I pondered what it would be like if Tim confessed to me that he was receiving love letters from a ghost. I would seriously consider having him committed. So where do I go from here?

I had already shared the experience with Flora as much as her schedule would permit and on Sunday evening she would leave for England.

Mildred Morrow would be my next choice. She taught the seventh-grade Sunday School and was the most-sincere Christian I had ever met. But would her faith be a roadblock to accepting what I was saying without considering it heresy? I would be putting our friendship on the line, and we hadn't really known each other that long. Would she believe me? For now I had to keep the lid on my secret and it wasn't easy.

The next morning was Sunday, and I would have a class to teach. I wouldn't dare share *this* experience with my class. It was just too far out, and I wasn't sure it would be good for fourteen-year-olds, not even those so enlightened, who first approached me with the idea of discussing reincarnation.

I awakened hours before the alarm to take advantage of the alone time to write. Dear John had a big surprise for me this morning. He started out by calling me **"Ellen."** He told me that in a previous life in England we had been married and had two children, Edward and Louisa, and told me I had been a good wife. We had lived in a place called *St. Joneswood*, London, England, and the word *Notting* (something I couldn't quite read) that I took it to be Nottingham. But Nottingham is not in London. It didn't make sense then, but many years later on a trip to England it would all come together.

One thing I must mention about automatic writing is that the spelling is awful. Most things are spelled as they are pronounced, so aside from no break between words, no *t's* are crossed nor *i's* dotted, making understanding what is being written a problem and subject to misunderstanding.

Now I had a new family and a new name. *John, Edward, and Louisa and myself as Ellen.* Although captivated by the idea and eager to learn more details, I had to wait. It was time to come back to 1972 and get my real-life family and myself ready for church.

After church I gave Flora a quick call and told her about Ellen, John, Edward, and Louisa and asked her to keep a watchful eye for a place called St. Joneswood while visiting England. She told me she was planning to try automatic writing at her first opportunity when she arrived in England. Then she asked me if I would ask John if he could tell her if she had also had a past life. I promised I would ask and wished her a wonderful trip, and wrote down the mailing address of her aunt Jenny where she would be staying. Suddenly I wished I could go with her. She was going to the country where I, as Ellen, had lived so long ago and who knows, she may even find St. Joneswood. I wasn't sure if the St was an abbreviation for Saint or Street.

While we were still on the phone John began to tell me about Flora's past life. It seems this was not the first time Flora and I had been friends. We had known each other before, I as Ellen Green Early and Flora as Jessica Inverness Jones. I loved Flora's name, Jessica Inverness Jones; it was much fancier than Ellen Early. The conversation abruptly ended when Tim entered the room.

A kaleidoscope of jigsaw pieces tumbled in my brain and occasionally one or two pieces would fall into place, giving me a peek into the past and into the future. There would be prophecy, poetry, a song, a glimpse of heaven, an eavesdropper into the Oval Room, stories of reincarnation, and more about my life as Ellen in England. To this day I am sometimes addressed as Ellen when I sit down to write automatically.

John continued to write me love letters and give me details of our family life. One day he wrote: **"Edward calls"** and then **"Mum, Edward here."** The words sent a chill climbing up my spine and a deep feeling of love filled my heart. *So* whenever the writing begins with *"Mum,"* I know I have a message from my beloved son and the words are warm and sweet. I asked if my daughter, Louisa, could write to me and was told that she had already been born and was living in Illinois. I was also told that my relationship with Louisa was not as loving as my relationship with my son Edward.

Perhaps it was just coincidence, but my eldest son, Dan, married a sweet young lady from Illinois. I often wondered if it could be Louisa, but the question may never be answered.

As my writing continued I received volumes of information regarding my past life as Ellen and also Flora's past life as Jessica. I transcribed some of it and mailed it to Flora in England. I also mailed many pages of the original writing. I hoped that Flora was by now able to write automatically. I felt intuitively that she was, and I couldn't wait to hear from her.

Since Dr. Ian Stevenson's book on reincarnation had first generated my interest in the subject, I decided to write to him, but this did not come easy. Who was I after all but an ordinary housewife who did not hold a college degree in anything, to write to such a learned man? "He probably won't even answer the letter," I thought. However, on February 24, I decided to give it a try. I wrote to him and told him the whole story. I was wrong about him; he was not some stogy old college professor who didn't associate with us common folk. We actually exchanged several letters that I have kept. Even though he had never known of anyone who had received messages from automatic writing from characters from a previous life, he was open to the idea.

Many years later I decided that it would be interesting to go to a regressionist and see if hypnosis would confirm or dispute the story of Ellen. On June 27, 1988, a friend and I drove to Virginia Beach to the home of Ted Sharp, a hypnotist who came highly recommended. After Mr. Sharp introduced me to his wife, she excused herself and went upstairs. I lay on my back on a chaise lounge and was covered with an afghan and put under hypnosis. While under hypnosis I *seemed* to recall a life as Ellen, but wasn't sure if it was a memory, wishful thinking, or my imagination. I wasn't even sure I was really *under* hypnosis. It was as if there were two parts of my brain arguing with each other: one telling an interesting story of Ellen and the other one whispering that it was all hogwash.

The first picture that came onto the screen of my mind was of bouncing brown curls sitting in front of me as we rode in an open horse-drawn carriage, first along a dirt road and then onto a cobblestone street. I, as Ellen, was on my way to boarding school and had mixed feelings about going. There was an indisputable smell of horses.

In brief, I learned that I, Ellen Green, was the daughter of a high-ranking military man and had a mother with whom I felt no bond. It was as if Ellen's mother were in deep grief, blamed that grief on her husband, and resented Ellen just for being alive. It seems that Ellen had a younger brother who was encouraged by his father to join the military at an early age and was killed in his first battle. Ellen's mother never forgave her husband and became mentally unbalanced.

Ellen's father had a good friend from childhood who had become an archaeologist and had worked for a number of years in Egypt. This friend had married an Egyptian woman who bore him a son. The three had returned to England, where they lived on property adjoining Ellen's family. Ellen became very attached to the Egyptian woman and her son. She loved hearing stories about the mysterious pyramids and the ancient history, but most of all she loved learning about their religious beliefs. Ellen also loved deeply the half Egyptian son, and they had planned to marry as soon as they were old enough. Ellen's mother hated the Egyptian woman and her son. Ellen was sent away to boarding school to keep her from being influenced by this lady and her "half-breed" son. Ellen wanted to get away from her abusive mother, but would sorely miss her Egyptian friends, especially the young man.

In boarding school Ellen formed a close circle of friends who read and discussed *"some theories told to her by her Egyptian friend that would be considered heresy by the Church of England and could get the girls into serious trouble."*

After a few years, Ellen's parents arranged her marriage to an older man of considerable wealth, John Early, and they moved to a place called St. Joneswood and had two children. Although Ellen was a good and faithful wife, her memory would bring back to life the evening she danced in an open field with her beloved, when they spoke of love and secretly planned a life together. Nothing specific was ever mentioned as to what became of the Egyptians except for a vague notion that they had returned to Egypt.

After becoming a widow, Ellen reunited with some of her old school friends who met secretly to continue their discussion of foreign religious beliefs. Such study was still forbidden by the church, and they could still be in serious trouble if caught. People were still being put to death if they were considered heretics by the church. The group vowed that if reincarnation was a reality, they would all come back to live in a place where they would be free to discuss openly anything they chose, *and I think we did!*

There are several things that lead me to believe that I was under hypnosis and the story was real. I was shocked to see the clock and realize that I had been lying motionless for almost four hours. I thought it had only been about fifteen or twenty minutes. At some point during the hypnosis I could smell bean soup cooking. Part of my mind became upset with Ted Sharp's wife for coming downstairs, walking through the room during my hypnosis, going into the kitchen, and making soup while I was having my session. When I came out of hypnosis, I discovered his wife had never come downstairs, and there was nothing cooking in the kitchen. The aroma of simmering bean soup was part of the hypnosis. Secondly, while still under hypnosis I learned that Ellen had some type of palsy. When she was dying, I experienced the pain she must have felt because my right leg, foot, arm, and hand gnarled up. The moment Ellen's soul left her body, my body straightened and I felt no more pain. Another interesting thing happened after I came out of hypnosis. Everything I tried to do had to be thought out. When writing my check I had to remember how to spell Carolyn. I had to ask my friend to drive because I wasn't sure I still knew how. I came back to being Carolyn but it was gradual and took several hours.

Chapter 5

Threshold of Heaven

Back to April 1972

In those early days of writing, for the most part, I received messages from John and Edward providing details of my life as Ellen. However, another entity appeared in my writing that identified himself as Rolling Guide who wrote inspirational messages of God's love for me and for all his children. Once he said: **"I give you nourishment for your soul. Use this to feed my lambs."**

It was also at this time that my cousin was dying of cancer. Everyone who knew her had been praying for her recovery. Her daughter was planning her wedding, and I knew my cousin wanted desperately to be a part of those wedding plans. However, God seemed to have turned a deaf ear to our prayers and her condition continued to deteriorate.

During one of my last visits with her, she said to me, "Carolyn, I know I look like a fat old bald-headed man and the pain is horrific, but I wouldn't mind that if I could only live."

Returning home from the hospital her words resonated in my mind bringing forth feelings of sadness and bewilderment. The inspirational messages from Rolling Guide spoke of a God who loved his children. How could a loving God allow my beloved cousin to die at just the time her daughter was planning her wedding? I decided to do some automatic writing and ask for an explanation. When I began to write, Rolling Guide identified himself and the following message appeared: **"Do not be dismayed, my child, for death is not real. Do not weep for the dead, for they yet live. Do not weep for the dying, for they are feeling the first pains of rebirth. Souls are matter and cannot be destroyed. Today you are as water and I am as vapor, tomorrow you will be as vapor and I as water."**

All of these new messages of reincarnation, God's love, and now this last message had to be kept inside me. I needed to share my experiences with someone. I needed a second opinion. With Flora out of the country and Tim out of the question, I gathered my courage and invited Mildred Morrow to come to my house for lunch on Monday, April 24, 1972, at 1:00 p.m.

In the meantime, I watched the incoming mail closely, anxiously awaiting a letter from Flora. At last her letter arrived. It was in a large overstuffed envelope covered almost completely with postage and bulging like a pregnant elephant. I had hoped to snatch it from the mailbox and read it without Tim noticing, but there he was staring at the oversized letter. Trying to hide my excitement I forced a casual voice. "Oh, how nice, a letter from Flora." Tim gave me a quizzical look and turned away to continue reading the newspaper. Oh great, I thought, Tim didn't notice the size of the letter.

Avoiding a jack rabbit start I tried to walk casually to the bedroom to read the letter. And there it was! Flora had indeed started doing automatic writing in England; there were twenty-one pages of automatic writing. Flora's handwriting isn't the easiest to read under any circumstance, but her automatic writing took quite a lot of effort and time. I spread the papers out on my bed trying to make sense of them.

Suddenly Tim poked his head in the door and asked, "What did Flora have to say?"

Snatching up the papers quickly I blurted out, "Nothing."

Tim gave me a quizzical look, eyeing the pile of papers and the badly ripped envelope lying on the bed. "Carolyn," he said, "that was the thickest letter I have ever seen and you are telling me it said *nothing*?"

"Well," I said, "Flora did have a lot to say about her trip."

Suspicion was written all over Tim's face. "Are you and Flora keeping secrets?" Tim asked.

"Yes, Tim," I sanctimoniously added, "I guess we are, but it's Flora's secret, not mine, and I promised not to tell anyone."

Tim shook his head, turned, and walked away.

The jig was up. I was caught! Now I would be forced to let Tim in on my secret writing or he would suspect something far worse. The moment I had dreaded for days had arrived. Scenarios played in my head: First, there was the scene where Tim didn't believe me; next there was a scene when he told me he thought I was losing my mind; then came the worst scenario of all, with an angry face, Tim would tell me to stop writing immediately. That would cause problems in our marriage, because I knew I couldn't give it up. I wouldn't allow Tim to dictate to me what I could or couldn't do with my time. Could automatic writing lead to divorce? Now even before I confessed to Tim about my writing, I was angry with him, anticipating his reaction. I would try to stall as long as possible.

It is now Monday morning, April 24, 1972. Mildred is coming for lunch, and I'm going to share my secret with her. The morning does not get off to a good start. I stumbled over my cat, broke an egg on the kitchen floor, spilled coffee on my best robe, sprayed deodorant on my hair, and all the while silly scenarios again played in my head. "She'll think I'm a kook and tell me that kooks who play around with the supernatural should *not* teach Sunday School."

When the house was empty, I decided to pray and write. As soon as the pen touched the paper a very clear message appeared: **"God is with you. Let me manage your language. Mildred will believe you. Mum, I will help her write today. You give her paper and pen and pray and we will do God's work today. Mildred will write on her first try. There will be words from Momma Morrow."**

A feeling of peace came over me as I tidied the house and prepared lunch. At least I felt at peace until the doorbell rang and my heart began to race. I took a few deep breaths and tried to act natural.

After lunch and a nice conversation about Sunday School and our wonderful students, I knew the time had come to tell all.

I must have said something right because *Mildred believed me!* I showed her the paper with the message I had received that morning, and she was astonished. She knew I had no way of knowing anything about her husband's mother or that almost everyone had called her *Momma Morrow*. She admitted that it had taken her a long time after she and Bill were married to call her mother-in-law *"Momma Morrow."*

Mildred told me that her mother-in-law had been a good Christian woman and that she had loved her dearly.

Mildred was now ready to try automatic writing. I gave her a pen and paper and we bowed our heads in prayer. I felt certain it would take at least fifteen or twenty minutes of her first session before the pen would actually begin to move and maybe much longer for there to be anything legible.

In less than a minute Mildred spoke my name in a choked whisper. I lifted my eyes and saw that her hand was trembling and the hair on her arms was standing on end. "Carolyn," she gasped, "the pen is moving." From across the table I could see words that were readable, but I dared not move for fear of interrupting the flow of her pen.

In a few minutes she pushed the paper across the table for me to read. I was amazed, her first writing was as clear as the message I had received that morning. It said, **"They are things you do not understand. They are not so lucky as you are. So do not deny it. Son of your Savior."**

My morning prophecy had come to pass. My language had seemed to be *managed* and my words convincing. Mildred had not only believed me, she had written on her *first try* and we were able to understand every word. My son from a bygone life had known of Mildred's mother-in-law and called her *Momma Morrow.* We were amazed. However, we were also puzzled by the words *"Son of your Savior"*; neither of us had ever heard that expression. Could this mean Jesus had a son?

In the days to come, Mildred set aside a time for writing every morning, and we called each other every day to share what we had received. Then came the day and the message that shocked both of us.

Mildred's sister-in-law, Hattie, was lying in a hospital in North Carolina being kept alive with feeding tubes and a breathing apparatus. She had been comatose for quite a while, and Mildred and her husband, Bill, had been told that the tubes would soon be removed and she would be allowed to die. The family was expecting the news of Hattie's death at any moment.

Mildred called me that morning to tell me that she had just received a message through her automatic writing and was sure that Hattie's soul was now in heaven. The message reads: **"6:55 a.m., God has taken her to his family. She is so**

thrilled. She is the happiest soul I have ever witnessed. She is loved by so many souls. She has been chosen by God to be with him. She has been the love of little children and loved by all my children. Yes, Yes, Go and seek. I am love. She is better off here. It is a place of great beauty and vibrant color. She loves it here. She loves God's family."

"What do you make of that?" Mildred asked after reading the message.

"I know I'm standing here with goose bumps on my arms," I replied. "And I know I'll never again mourn the death of a Christian."

Mildred and I were convinced that at any moment the call would come notifying her of Hattie's passing. We were wrong! A few days later word arrived from North Carolina that Hattie had come out of her coma, and with a strength no one thought she had, pulled all the tubes from her body. The doctor decided not to replace her life support and allow nature to take its course. But nature took a different course that left everyone dumbfounded. Hattie Roseman had made a complete recovery! In a matter of only a few weeks she was released from the hospital and was at home doing her housework. It was a miracle! But it seemed to prove that Mildred's writing had been mistaken. Coupled with some of the things that had been coming through Flora's writing, our doubts about the value of automatic writing were increasing and our enthusiasm for it wavering.

However, it was not until the fall of 1972 that the whole story of Hattie's illness came to light. Bill and Mildred drove to North Carolina to attend a family reunion and found Hattie well and happy, helping with the preparations for the family gathering. Just three months after her close brush with death, this seventy-five-year-old lady was strong and active.

Toward evening when Mildred and Hattie found a few quiet moments away from the crowd, Hattie confided to Mildred that during her illness, she felt that she had actually died and gone to heaven. She asked Mildred to promise her that if she ever got that sick again to tell her family not to pray for her recovery, she didn't want to come back. Her description of her experience was so close to the words that appeared in Mildred's automatic writing that it left Mildred in awe.

I asked Mildred to ask Hattie if she would be willing to put her story in a letter for me. In February 1973, she did. The letter begins on page 2; page 1 was of a personal nature to Mildred.

2

you asked me if I mined to write about my illness and miraculous recovery. no it dosent make me nervous. it does make me feel very humble. it dosen't seem, as if I'm worthy to be a good chanel for gods power to be manifested through. but I have prayd, and thought so much of why was I stricken so suddenly. and then, not remember any thing of the pain or people, nor examinations. it just seems as if god kept my spirit, of which we are, free from knowledge of ~~consciousness~~ consciouness of what was happening. I have become satisfied, that the illness was for a purpose. to glorify god. that through the "prayers" of many people. god could show his praying people, that their prayers does have power through him. you wanted to know when I intered the hospital, it was april 9, and discharged may 29. and except for the last eight or ten days all is oblivian. as to what you could call the absent of knowledge I don't know. they said I would talk and seemed to know most of the time what I was saying.

3

I am sure I didn't know. or I Would have Not changed my mind as to the food. and some other things. any way. Dr. Caldwell said they thought they were going to loose me for Several Days, but by some miracle, I suddenly changed. Mildred its hard to write my feelings. but I'll try. I had the sence of seeing a place of peace. there was the faces of people I had known, Some Seemed to be near some farther away all along the Sands of a place, a river bank, though I Saw No Water. and No end of land. just space, and to the left, there was a place with Colors, Colors, in Shapes i've never Saw. also turning golden, Swords, I thought this looks like the, Swords at the garden of Eden. No sound, nothing moving except these Colors and Swords. then I Seemed to have asked, Why don't we go in. and a Voice said, the time is Not ready to enter. thats all. When I Came to my Self, (I said at first i've come back) its a little hazy. but I Was Sorry I Was back. for a little while. I had to lay there and Wonder why god had sent me back. I

4

dident tell any one, what I thought. I thought it would make them feel bad. So I got to studying it all over. and now I feel that I let the people who prayd and sat with me down, yes and jesus also. for I dident let his power serve them. So I asked his forgiveness, now I'm telling what his holy spirit and power through the spirit will do. we have to tell others, in every way and every place. I do feel that god took me in the spirit to once look the outer courts of heaven, and to tell others there is no fear in death, for there is no death of the spirit. it was just like slipping away, from one life to another. not even darkness. oh I guess I could go on and on. about that happiness. So satisfied. no fear. just wonderment.

The doctors, decided not to operate, because I started having a high temp. and the same said he wouldent operate, me not having the will to live. (gods hand) then when I was able for it. they decided. to let nature heal. really they never seemed to have a clear diagnosis.

6

they haven't seemed to fully to understand. all the illness. I do know that gods hand was in it, and the only reason, I have been able to come up with, is, that many people can be blessed by it, as well as my self. not that I am so worthy. But he knows I am a talker ha and now I can talk for him, more & more. With his help. what he leads me to say. Ill say. it may not be often. but I want to speak the truth. I can't do it. if I try to go before him. Well I think its time for me to stop now. I hope Ive been of some help to Carolyn. it seems strange, but things have been happening the last few weeks. that have drawn me out, I think god has a time and way. To tell of his love. I would like to see you when you come home. I am happy for Sarah. I know she has had a long hard. road. being mother and father. I just pray their lives will be a happy one. tell all Hello. so glad Rosemary is able to go to work. and hope Bill will not get down again. Love to all

Hattie

Years later I learned that Hattie's experience was not unique, it is called NDE (Near Death Experience) and there have been thousands recorded all over the world. But in 1972 we didn't know about NDE; for Mildred, for me, and for Hattie, it was the first time any of us had heard of anyone going to heaven using a roundtrip ticket.

U.S. POSTAL SERV. PM 21 FEB 1973

EISENHOWER USA 8c

Mrs G. G. Morrow
5102 W. Lanham Dr.,
Hyattsville, Md. 2078

Chapter 6

Flora Returns

May 1972

I gathered my bundle of papers and drove to Flora's house. She had just returned from England and there was much to discuss and share. More interesting things had happened to me in the last few weeks than at any other time in my life. I was euphoric!

We sat at her table in front of the large picture window as we had done so many times before but this was different. There was so much "show and tell" that we hardly knew where to begin. I told Flora that Mildred was also doing automatic writing (although at this time the full story of Hattie was unknown).

I was anxious to learn more about Flora's experiences with automatic writing in England. I had gathered from her letters and samples of her writing that there was something ominous and frightening, and although I was both puzzled and concerned by the story she was telling me, I was most of all intrigued. I was also curious about some of the material contained in her letters to me. I asked her to start from the first phone call from me about the writing and bring me up-to-date on her experiences.

April 1972, Summary of Flora's Initiation into Automatic Writing in Her Own Words

Opened half-packed suitcases covered our king-sized bed in our mini-sized bedroom. Assorted clothes hung from every available door, doorknob, and chair back. Even my dog, Cleo, couldn't find a comfortable spot to lie down to watch me pack.

The phone chimed again. "I hope it's Carolyn with another message," I thought. Each of her messages thrust us deeper into our latest endeavor, automatic writing.

Feeling like schoolgirls filled with delicious new secrets, Carolyn and I were in no mood for skeptical negative, ambiguous comments from our husbands, so we did not confide our intriguing new project in them. Consequently, our telephone conspiracy began. Conversations laced with coded speech and the four words that would become a byword between us, "I have a message."

Eagerly, I climbed over the suitcases, stretched across the bed, and reached for the phone. Taking a chance it was Carolyn, I trilled *"Helloooo"* It was Carolyn, her voice vibrant with excitement, hushed by wonder, but so controlled that I thought she was going to strangle on the words, "I have a message."

But then, Carolyn the cool, methodical, the analytic, mercurially became Carolyn the babbler. Her control suddenly unleashed words that spilled out and came popping through the telephone wires. "I just received another message from John. He wrote: **'John here, please remember me. We had children, Edward and Louisa. Ellen you were a good woman.'**"

I couldn't believe it, yet I did believe it. "I feel strange," I said, "like I'm in on something I shouldn't be."

"Who sent this message, and where was this John?"

Carolyn was as bewildered as I.

"Carolyn," I said, "write again and see what happens."

Carolyn told me the pen was moving slowly and she read each letter as it appeared on the paper. **"J-e.s.s.i.c.a. Flora is Jessica"** she spelled it out to me.

I sat upright on the bed. The hair on my arms stood on end, and I'm sure my mouth was hanging open. "What?" I whispered incredulously,

"Wait," Carolyn gagged, "there is more. It looks like a date: **"1-8-0-0 J-e-s-s-I-c-a- I-n-v-e-r-n-e-s-s- J-o-n-e-s Joneswater, no, Joneswood."**

I, Flora Cameron Young May, had been Jessica Inverness Jones in the 1800s. What a message!

I was anxious for Carolyn to continue writing, but she whispered, "Tim just came in" and her tone changed to one of light good humor and her innocent good-bye could not have aroused Tim's suspicions. "Have a good trip."

"I'll write and let you know what's happening here," she said matter-of-factly.

I gave her my aunt Jenny's address in England, and I told her I would try automatic writing at my first opportunity when I arrive in England. I sat on the edge of the bed, our conversation whirling around in my head. "Was this really happening?" I asked myself. "Had we opened Pandora's Jar?" I decided my first effort would be on the plane.

How could I have known when I left on my trip to England and Scotland that my future memories of this marvelous trip would not only include my Scottish relatives, but intangible beings claiming kinship, namely, Joseph, Steven, and the evil Richard.

My writing was very different from Carolyn's. I did not receive any beautiful, spiritual messages. The majority of my writing manifested itself in hostile and lying messages, threats of rape and vulgar four-letter words. I didn't want my husband to see them and I certainly did not want my aunt Jenny to see them, so I tore the pages into small pieces, put them into an envelope and then threw them away in a trash can when we were out sightseeing.

During all those weeks in England and Scotland, I was simultaneously fascinated, curious and frightened, but most of all I was shaken by the thought that I was so unworthy that I only attracted evil spirits. I examined my life and wondered what I did that was so terrible that the enchanting messages that Carolyn received were denied me. However, invariably intermingled with the miserable messages were the words *"Jesus loves you."*

One morning I wrote, "Why do I have Richard when he is such a low-level spirit? Don't I deserve a spirit on a high level?"

The answer (apparently from Richard) was: **"Realize Good is lost, realize Richard is feared by spirits read nnnnn. He is irradiating evil and I love radiating evil, realize Good is a parrot of rudeness."**

I must have asked, "Is Richard a part of my mind?" The answer was, **"Yes, Richard is part of your mind. Richard loves you."**

I don't know how I responded in my mind, but Richard wrote, **"Life is funny lover girl. It is a nothing Blace (place) nowhere. Believe me Richard is bad renation (Richard's spelling) Believe me Richard is a bad reincarnation of Richard Brown."** No wonder I felt like a loser!

Sometime during the first week in London, I discovered that I could write with my finger. I could lay my hand on any flat surface and my finger would begin to write. Later I received automatic drawings that amazed me. I am not an artist and I could not have drawn these pictures consciously. Much later, after I was home in Maryland, I began to receive music notes. Also in the months after I returned home to Maryland, I received many messages hostile in nature, lies and bad news about my family. But as time went by I received fewer and fewer messages, just crazy things and I never figured out what they meant. For example, **"Roses from Boston"**; these words came to me countless times. I was bored by this time. I didn't have the patience to sit and wait for a decent message that would never manifest itself.

That was the end of my experience with automatic writing. However, I have always enjoyed Carolyn's beautiful messages that come to her frequently, a constant amazement to all who read them.

Summer of 1972, Photo of Roaring Twenties Party. Mike May in Keystone Cop costume, Flora and Carolyn as flappers, delivering invitations in the form of subpoenas. The sign on the car reads “The Touch-Me-Knots.”

Chapter 7

Searching the Scriptures

Increasingly, automatic writing was becoming the vortex of my existence, and I wasn't sure everything it was pulling in was good. Mildred had received that message about Hattie and we thought at the time it was a lie, and I sometimes spent hours writing and could hardly read any of it. However, the most frightening messages came through Flora. Why Flora? She is a good person, so why would God allow evil spirits to attack her? It made no sense.

I decided that before I ventured further into the unknown I needed to learn to meditate. I followed instructions described in Ruth Montgomery's book with neck exercises and breathing. I also prayed for a spiritual cleansing. I asked that all negative thoughts and false beliefs be purged from my consciousness to allow my spirit to fill with God's love and Truth. I had a hard time at first getting into the meditative mode because my mind continually reminded me of all the things I *should* be doing. I made gradual progress and finally came to enjoy meditation.

Then a funny thing happened. I noticed that when I woke up something was missing. No sneezes! After nearly thirty years of awakening to the sound of my own sneezes, they were suddenly gone. I had not given a thought to asking for a healing, it just happened. Furthermore, during the years that followed when meditation was a part of my daily ritual, I never caught a cold or one of those pesky viruses going through the community. I thought my health had been good before, but now I had more energy than I had ever had in my life. I went for twenty years without a cold, allergy, or intestinal virus.

I also decided to read the New Testament, *Good News for Modern Man*, from start to finish as if I had never before seen it, trying to avoid old interpretations from various ministers and Sunday School teachers. I wanted to know if anything resembling reincarnation was ever mentioned. Flora and I had read that reincarnation had been a part of Christianity until a pope declared it an untruth. I was shocked when I reached the 11th chapter of Matthew verse 10 through 15 and read: *For John is the one of whom the scripture says: "Here is my messenger, says God; I will send him ahead of you to open the way for you." Remember this! John the Baptist is greater than any man who has ever lived. But he who is least in the Kingdom of heaven is greater than he. From the time John preached his message until this very day the Kingdom of heaven has suffered violent attacks and violent men try to seize it. All the prophets and the Law of Moses, until the time of John, spoke about the Kingdom; and if you are willing to believe their message, JOHN IS ELIJAH, whose coming was predicted. Listen, then, if you have ears!* Then again in Matthew 17: 10-13: *"When the disciples asked Jesus, 'Why do the teachers of the Law say that Elijah has to come first?' 'Elijah does indeed come first,' answered Jesus, 'and he will get everything ready. But I tell you this: Elijah HAS come and people did not recognize him, but treated him just as they pleased. In the same way the Son of Man will also be mistreated by them." Then the disciples understood that he was talking to them about John the Baptist."*

These words came from the mouth of Jesus Christ. Could it be any clearer? It doesn't say John the Baptist was "doing the work of" Elijah, Jesus said *"JOHN IS ELIJAH."* For me, that was all the confirmation I needed to convince me that the Truth for which I had prayed and searched had been in the scriptures all along but I had accepted the interpretation of others.

As I read further I came to a story that is very familiar to everyone, the story of the woman at the well who was caught committing adultery. This has to be one of the most-quoted scriptures in the entire Bible. John 8, verses 1 through 11: *"Then everyone went home, but Jesus went to the Mount of Olives. Early the next morning he went back to the temple. The whole crowd gathered around him and he sat down and began to teach them. The teachers of the Law and the Pharisees brought in a woman who had been caught committing adultery, and made her stand before them all. 'Teacher,' they said to Jesus, 'this woman was caught in the very act of committing adultery. In our Law Moses gave a commandment that such a woman must be stoned to death. Now, what do you say?' They said this to trap him, so they could accuse him. BUT JESUS BENT OVER AND WROTE ON THE GROUND WITH HIS*

FINGER. As they stood there asking questions, he straightened up and said to them, WHICH EVER AMONG YOU WHO IS WITHOUT SIN, LET HIM THROW THE FIRST STONE AT HER. Then He BENT OVER AGAIN AND WROTE ON THE GROUND." After the people left, Jesus said, *"Go, but sin no more."*

Could Jesus have been doing automatic writing? Many times Jesus said, "it is not me, but my Father who does these works." Why did Jesus find it necessary to *write in the sand with his finger* before he spoke? Might He have been seeking help from his heavenly Father?

Suddenly reincarnation and automatic writing no longer felt like heresy. With a little different interpretation in the beginning when the scriptures were incorporated into the Bible, who knows, all Christians could have accepted reincarnation and used automatic writing to communicate with the Divine.

I thought of how Flora, like Jesus, could write with her finger on any flat surface. However, unlike Jesus, Flora's messages were *not* from the Divine; she was under attack by a sinister entity named Richard. Was this what was meant in the scriptures in Matthew 11, *"the Kingdom of Heaven has suffered violent attacks and violent men try to seize it?"* If, as it states in the Bible, our bodies are the Temple of God, and if that Temple is the Kingdom of Heaven, Jesus could have been describing exactly what was happening to Flora.

A new book entitled *The Exorcist* was becoming a best seller, and there was a movie about to be released by the same name. I heard that the book was based on a real case that took place not too far from where we were living. I hadn't read the book, but I had read accounts of the real case. Could an evil entity or devil take over someone's body as was alleged in the true case? Could this happen to Flora? I knew very little about such occurrences, but I was sure Flora was strong enough to withstand the attacks. But why should she have to? We needed to exorcise Richard, and we needed to do it now!

Chapter 8

The Exorcism of Richard

For clergy throughout the ages, from biblical times until the latest case, on which *The Exorcist* was based, exorcism has been a ritual practiced in Christian religion. But Flora and I were not clergy, let alone exorcists. How could we go about ridding Flora of this evil entity who called himself Richard?

My first thought was to tell him to go back to hell from whence he came, and never enter our lives again, be it through our automatic writing or another channel ... or else we would sick God on him. When I expressed my idea, Flora and I cracked up with laughter even though we knew this was serious business.

Besides, this approach might allow Richard to resurface and perhaps torment some other unsuspecting mortal. So we prayed for his soul. We took turns expressing our concern for Richard and asking that God would heal his soul with the power of Love. We also thanked Richard for being a messenger that brought us a Truth we needed to know, that not all spirit entities are angels and that we perhaps needed to be more cautious before experimenting with what some would call the supernatural.

We continued to say a few words and Flora would write. From her writing it was obvious that Richard was not willing to leave without a fight. Through Flora he cursed us and we laughed at him. Then we prayed for his forgiveness from God and from ourselves. In the end, we felt more sympathy for Richard than we felt fear or anger. Poor Richard was a lost and miserable soul who needed to find God and we told him that. At last he left, saying to Flora, **"Goodbye, I hope you have a miserable life"** and Richard was never heard from again.

Many times over the years I questioned in my mind why Richard had attacked Flora while my writing, though sometimes embarrassing, was never vulgar. It certainly wasn't because I was a better person than Flora. We wondered if it was because she hadn't been in a good place to devote a great deal of time to meditation and prayer before she tried to write. If I had received a threat, or so much as one curse word, I would not have given "them" a chance for a second. I concluded that Flora was chosen to receive the profane because she was strong enough to handle it, and we both needed to know that this sort of thing exists. In the end, I think Richard was a messenger from God, sent to tell us that our *"kingdom of God within, our body temple"* can suffer violent attack, as it says in the scripture but God within us is strong, strong enough to prevail over the enemies of our soul.

Chapter 9

Poetry

In 1972, the book, *The Exorcist*, was frightening everyone. In 1973 a movie was made based on the book that was even more frightening. Anything to do with what was defined as *supernatural* was labeled "Satanic" and I must admit after the Richard experience, we were questioning the source of our writing. Were we fooling around with something we oughtn't? Although most of our writing dealt with reincarnation, there were some other messages of interest.

The first words of warning or prophecy came in a message through me directed to Flora regarding her daughter, and it turned out to be quite beneficial. The message reads: **"Barbara's lawyer is Not looking out for her best interest. Find another who will."** When I read the message to Flora she told me that Barbara had no reason to hire a lawyer so we assumed *they* must have been referring to another person named Barbara. We were mystified until two days later when Barbara came to visit Flora to tell her that she was planning to divorce her husband and had consulted a lawyer. Flora advised Barbara to find another lawyer and she did. Later a friend told Barbara that she was glad she did not hire the first lawyer because he had a bad reputation.

That piece of unsolicited advice not only helped Barbara escape a potential problem, but also told Flora and me that there were things that we could not have known in our subconscious mind coming through us in the form of automatic writing messages. This was the first of many messages that made no sense at the time it was written, but in the days, weeks, or months that followed proved all too true. If all automatic writing were Satanic, why would Satan want to *help* Barbara?

On September 9, 1972, I received the following message: **"We have a birthday gift for you,"** *and* in less than ten minutes wrote the following:

TRUTH

Truth haunts us like a beautiful song, written long ago
Music of a forgotten past, in a life we used to know
We've shrouded her in veils of doubt
And so she walks in scorn
With ridicule her companion, we neither weep nor mourn
She comes so close and yet so far, as we see her pass us by
For in the blindness of our mind, we mistake her for a lie

As far as great poetry is concerned, I know this doesn't fall into the Shakespeare or Longfellow category, but it was written automatically in about six or eight minutes without a break. It wasn't until I read it aloud to Flora that we discovered it rhymed.

The poem "Truth" was followed in a few days by one entitled "Lies," and came in less than two minutes; I couldn't make up a nursery rhyme that fast. It wrote:

LIES

Lies come dressed in beauty
Like the purity of snow
Falling as if from heaven
So how shall mortals know?
Lies with facades of Truth
Truth with facades of lies
The masquerade goes whirling by
Too fast for human eyes

On September 20, 1972, I received another gift of poetry entitled "Memory":

MEMORY

Memory is shadow in a dimly lighted room
Carried on the breath of past
Stirred by its perfume
There's a door that is not open
Yet neither will it close
Is there a world beyond that door
Where memory freely flows?

The light of Truth holds the key
To reveal that sacred spot
Of a time not quite remembered
Yet never quite forgot
Haunting bits of memory
In a hushed and whispered cry
Never can they live again
But never truly die

After I read the words and discovered it was another poem, I asked if the writer had a name. My source wrote: **"George Darby Moss."**

We looked up the name in the encyclopedia and found nothing. Have you ever heard of him? If so, let me know.

Many years later Flora made and gave me a counter cross stitch of the poem "Memory." It hangs in my bedroom and is one of my most treasured possessions and a constant reminder of the awe and wonder I felt in those early days of automatic writing.

Flora, Mildred, and I also reached another decision. We had to tell our husbands about the writing. Now at least I had something other than love letters from a ghost to show Tim. The poetry and the prophecy about Barbara would make the telling a bit easier.

And there was someone else we needed to confront with the details of our secret: a Christian minister. Our own minister was out of the question. After all, we were teachers of the seventh, eighth, and ninth grades, composing 90 percent of the junior department of our church. Our minister had a responsibility to the board of directors, and our secret would place him in an awkward position. We had to find another minister from another area with whom we could entrust our secret, someone we dared to tell. We finally thought of a minister who lived many miles from us who had no affiliation with our church.

I don't know which I dreaded most, telling Tim or confronting a Christian minister. But the three of us knew what we had to do, and the three of us had to muster the courage to do it and do it soon.

Chapter 10
Blazing Fires

Three husbands with three different reactions. I guess that should have surprised no one, but it did.

I told Tim I had something important to discuss with him at a time when the children were out of the house. When I thought the time was right, I gathered some of my writing, selectively of course, and we sat at the kitchen table. I explained that a couple of my Sunday School students had asked about reincarnation, told him about the books I had read, that included Dr. Ian Stevenson's thesis on reincarnation and Ruth Montgomery's *Search for Truth*. I told him that I had read about automatic writing in Ruth Montgomery's book, told him that I had tried it and it worked. Tim just sat there quietly and listened. No shock, no disbelief, no reaction whatsoever. He accepted everything I said because *I* said it. He believed me, but displayed no interest nor did he ask a single question. He did ask me to ask "my friends" who would win the football game. I tried to write hoping there would be something that would stimulate his interest, but "my friends" refused to answer.

My husband had greeted my exciting news with acceptance and disinterest. All this time I was afraid to tell him for fear he wouldn't believe me or that it would upset him to the point that he would ask me to quit. This was not the reaction I expected. In spite of all the prophecies that came to pass, in spite of all the inspirational messages, in spite of how much it changed my way of thinking, he has remained accepting but disinterested. Even now, after all these years, I tell him something that came in the writing, and he'll say, "that's nice" or "that's interesting" and quickly change the subject.

Mildred's husband, Bill, reacted more in the way I had expected from Tim. It made him feel uneasy and he told her so. Although he did not specifically ask her to quit, Mildred knew that Bill disapproved and over time she gave up writing.

However, she has never failed to mention in her annual Christmas letter how much that experience meant to her and how she will never forget the wonderful spiritual adventure we shared so long ago.

Flora's husband, Mike, is Catholic and, of course, reincarnation is not accepted in Catholic doctrine. However, he had read some of Flora's books and was open to the possibility. He not only accepted the idea of automatic writing, he tried it. He sometimes watched as Flora's pen moved about the paper creating drawings. One day as Mike watched from across the table Flora's pen began to draw. Flora told Mike that she was getting tired of this because it looked like scribble. Mike encouraged her to continue, telling her she was drawing upside down and please don't stop. Flora was astonished when she turned the paper around, she found a picture she didn't know she was drawing.

basis for youth
Carolyn

Chapter 10: Blazing Fires

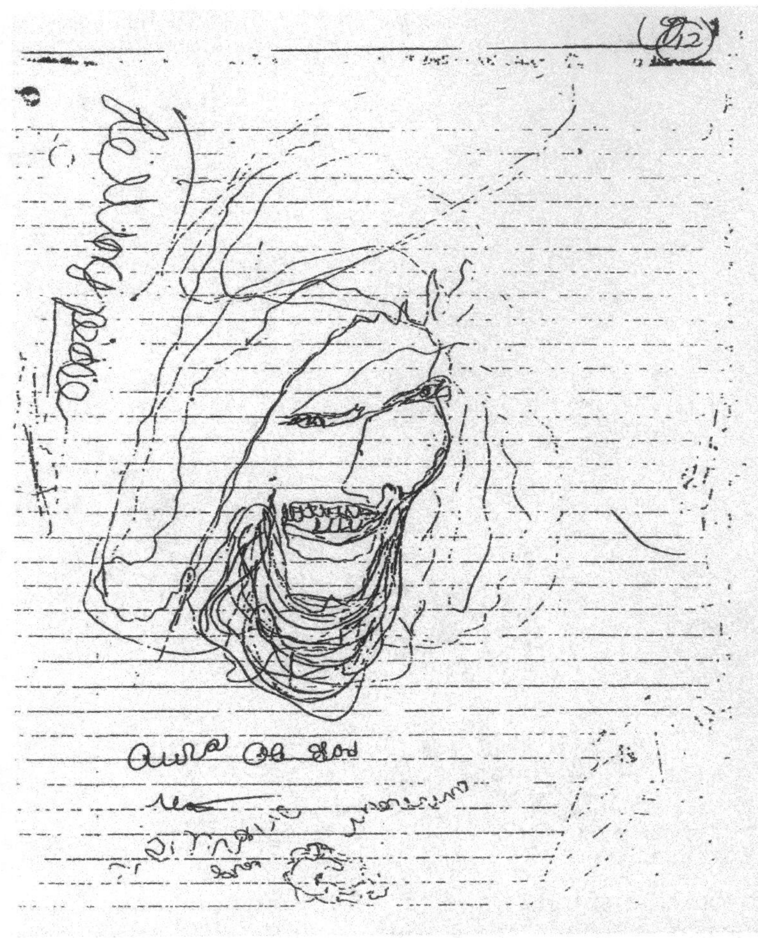

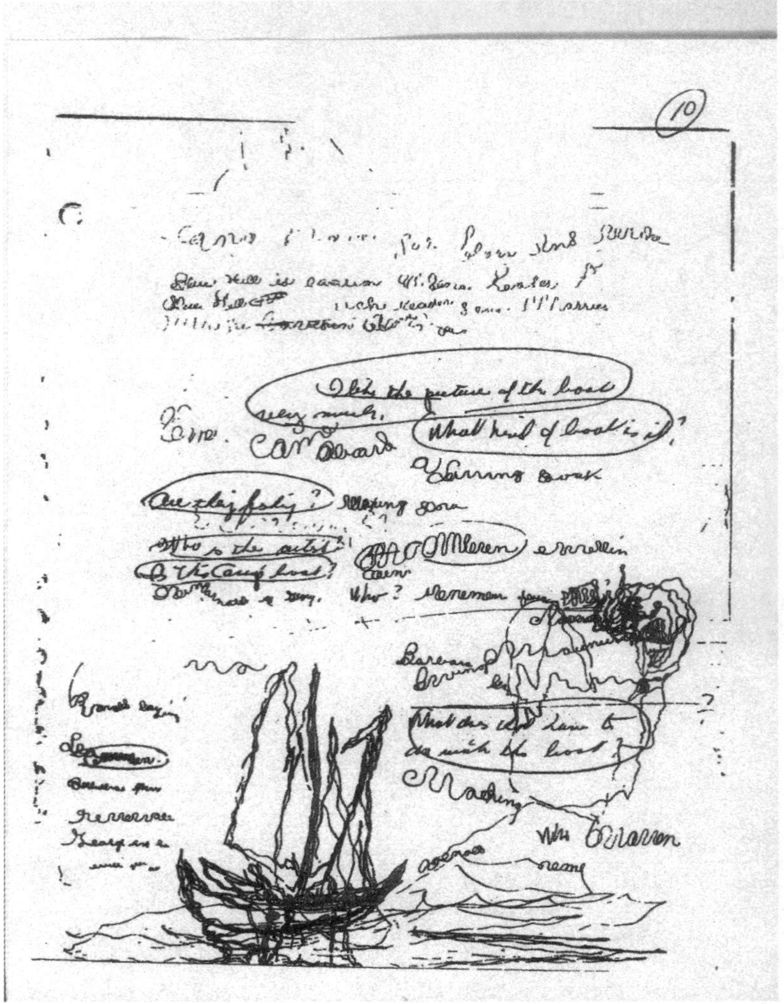

Throughout the summer and into fall, our notebooks filled with messages from the world beyond, stimulating our interest and curiosity. What would a member of the clergy think of our experiences? I had the feeling that if the clergy would be completely honest with us and with themselves, they would admit to us that many of them have received inspirational messages from exactly the same source, even though they may well label what we were doing as witchcraft or worse.

We decided to make an appointment with a Christian minister we knew and trusted and who knew and trusted us. We chose one far from home who was not affiliated with our church and wrote him to set up an appointment. My letter was dated October 30, 1972, and our appointment was scheduled for mid-November.

The long drive was filled with "what if's" and concern that we might be putting the minister on the spot. We knew he wouldn't think we had gotten together, concocted a big lie, and brought it to him; he knew us better than that. But how would he accept what we were about to unload on him? People come to ministers for advice all the time with a myriad of personal problems, but I doubt if three Sunday School teachers who were experimenting with the supernatural had ever confronted him. We typed out some of the beautiful prayers, poetry, and stories of our previous lives and brought along Flora's drawings.

When we finally arrived and exchanged the usual greetings, my knees began to knock and my hand quivered. After all the mental rehearsing, I was at a loss for words on how to begin. I wanted to defer to Mildred or Flora but as they said, "you started this, you have to tell him," and so I began.

The reverend sat expressionless as I related to him our experiences with automatic writing. There was no shock, no accusations of heresy or condescending holier-than-thou attitude, he just sat and listened without comment. I wondered if ministers are taught in theology class to sit quietly and listen without allowing facial expression or body language to betray their emotions.

He said he believed us, but added that he had never heard of automatic writing. Although he was well read, he had never read Edgar Casey or anything else about reincarnation but promised to do so. He even promised to try automatic writing.

On our drive home, we discussed the meeting and all concluded that we hadn't a clue as to what the minister had thought of the three Sunday School teachers who had confronted and challenged him to try something that could easily be labeled supernatural and contrary to the theology to which he had devoted most of his life. We couldn't wait to hear from him after he read the books from the list we gave him and tried automatic writing as promised. I was naive enough to be convinced that a man with his intellect and education would succeed in doing automatic writing and come up with some wonderful things to share with us.

But we didn't want to wait to hear from him. We would check with our spirit friends and find out exactly what the minister had thought of our visit and check to see if he had attempted automatic writing. However, my spiritual guides completely ignored my questions. There was not a word about the reverend, nothing about his feelings regarding our visit, and nothing about whether or not he had tried automatic writing. I was frustrated and a little angry that my spirit guides would be so unresponsive to my questions.

In fact, on November 27, after asking questions about the minister's reactions to our visit, I received the following message:

"Blazing fires, blazing fires, Louziana, clock strikes ten the fires begin. skyscraper we've blamed a group ... seven spirits perish."

I was asking about the reverend and my spirit guides were telling me about a fire in Louisiana and even misspelled Louisiana. I was disgusted and called Flora to tell her. We agreed that there were fires in Louisiana every day, and in order for there to be any validity in my writing, the fire would have to make headlines in the Washington newspapers. When we picked up our newspaper on the morning of November 30, 1972, we were astounded. This is what we saw:

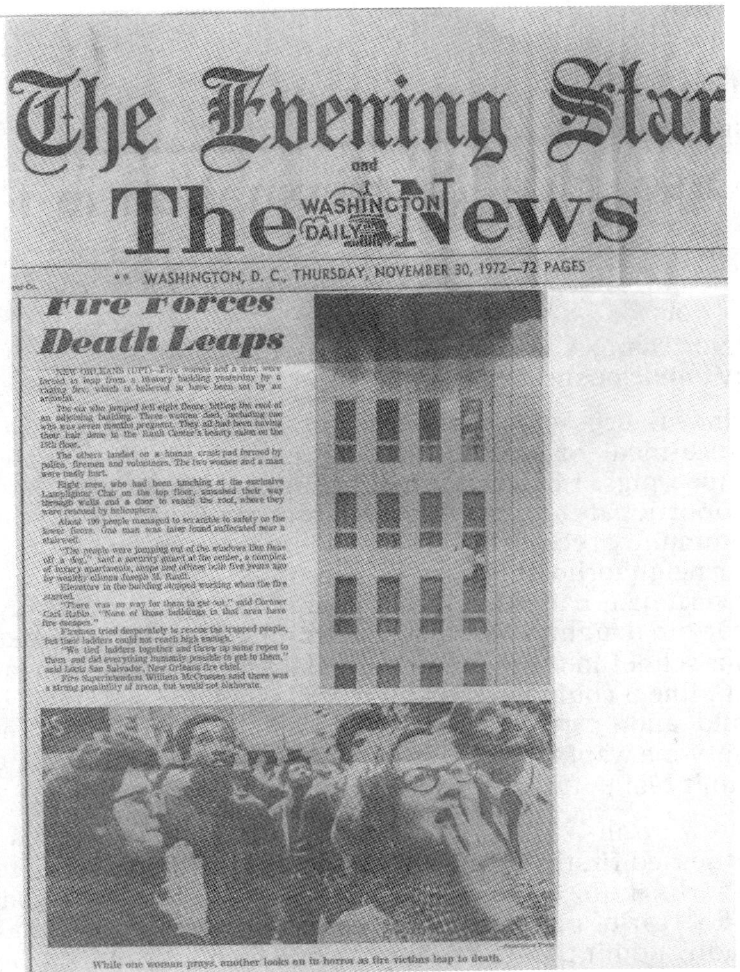

The Evening Star and The Washington Daily News

WASHINGTON, D. C., THURSDAY, NOVEMBER 30, 1972—72 PAGES

Fire Forces Death Leaps

NEW ORLEANS (UPI)—Five women and a man were forced to leap from a 16-story building yesterday by a raging fire, which is believed to have been set by an arsonist.

The six who jumped fell eight floors, hitting the roof of an adjoining building. Three women died, including one who was seven months pregnant. They all had been having their hair done in the Rault Center's beauty salon on the 15th floor.

The others landed on a human crash pad formed by police, firemen and volunteers. The two women and a man were badly hurt.

Eight men, who had been lunching at the exclusive Lamplighter Club on the top floor, smashed their way through walls and a door to reach the roof, where they were rescued by helicopters.

About 100 people managed to scramble to safety on the lower floors. One man was later found suffocated near a stairwell.

"The people were jumping out of the windows like fleas off a dog," said a security guard at the center, a complex of luxury apartments, shops and offices built five years ago by wealthy oilman Joseph M. Rault.

Elevators in the building stopped working when the fire started.

"There was no way for them to get out," said Coroner Carl Rabin. "None of those buildings in that area have fire escapes."

Firemen tried desperately to rescue the trapped people, but their ladders could not reach high enough.

"We tied ladders together and threw up some ropes to them and did everything humanly possible to get to them," said Louis San Salvador, New Orleans fire chief.

Fire Superintendent William McCrossen said there was a strong possibility of arson, but would not elaborate.

While one woman prays, another looks on in horror as fire victims leap to death.

The Washington Star and the Washington Daily News

November 30, 1972

"FIRE FORCES DEATH LEAPS"

"New Orleans, (UPI) Five women and a man were forced to leap from a 16 story building yesterday by a *'raging fire'* which is believed to have been set by arsonists." My writing said seven had perished, the paper said six. However, as we read further, we discovered that one woman was seven months pregnant.

Chapter 11
Bluebirds Will Lead You
Oval Room Will Tell

Major changes were in store in my life, not only from within my consciousness but from within my community. Bussing!

Prince George's County, Maryland, was initiating a social and educational experiment, and I felt my children were the guinea pigs. I lived in a racially mixed community that was proportionate to that of the county, and the schools in our community reflected the same. I felt there was no problem in our neighborhood. However, county officials and the federal government had other ideas. There were plans to bus my six-year-old daughter for forty-five minutes each way to take her to a school in a predominately black neighborhood near the D.C. line. I could not see where that would help a single black child, and I certainly didn't think it would help *my* little girl. Everyone wants what's best for *his or her own* children, and I didn't feel that this was best for mine.

I grew up in Washington, D.C., in the 1930s and 1940s, and witnessed firsthand the mass exodus of white families to the suburbs in the 1950s. My family was a part of that exodus. I had a fear of blacks in mass, especially young black males. I readily admit that is a prejudice of which I was guilty. Before blacks moved into my blue-collar neighborhood crime was rare.

After my neighborhood became predominately black, crime went way up, and I felt uncomfortable walking to the corner to mail a letter. Black youths congregated on the corner across the street and shouted vulgarities and threats of what they would like to do to "a white girl." If their shouts were intended to frighten me they succeeded.

Our apartment building was broken into three times in the year before my parents moved. Once I awakened to see a black arm cutting the screen of our back porch and unlatching the door. My father chased the man up the back alley with a large monkey wrench, and I followed close behind, afraid my father would be hurt. We watched as the man jumped into a car we could not afford and drove away. To a young teenage girl this was frightening. I didn't hate anyone and certainly wished him or her no harm, but I was afraid to venture into a predominately black neighborhood, let alone live in one again. It took many years and much help from my spirit guides to overcome this fear and prejudice, but at this time in the 1970s this fear remained.

My oldest son was in high school and had friends of both races who were always welcome in our home. However, there was racial trouble brewing in their high school, and for the first time I heard the term "rent a cop." To me it was shocking that a school needed a policeman to maintain order. The members of my son's racially mixed football team were a close-knit group who tried to come up with ideas that would promote racial harmony. I wasn't worried about my son's safety; he got along well with both races and was big and strong enough to take care of himself.

My middle son was in junior high and was not on the list to be bussed out of the community. However, blacks were being bussed in. As a result of this bussing, his class in pre-algebra had to go back to their multiplication tables. My son was losing interest in school and his grades reflected that disinterest. I felt the solution was to give those who needed to learn their multiplication tables private tutoring rather than require those who already knew their multiplication tables to tread water until the others caught up.

But it was my daughter's situation that tipped the scales. I could remember the taunts of the black boys on the corner in Washington, and I didn't want her to suffer the same humiliation or worse. We tried to find a private school for all three of our children, but private schools filled up quickly when bussing was first proposed. It would also have been a financial hardship to pay private school tuition for three children. The choice was fight or flight. We tried to fight, but our pleas were stifled with accusations of racism. So for the second time my family chose flight.

However, that flight brought pain. We had lived in the same community for more than seventeen years and our roots had grown deep. My husband coached football for the Lanham Boys and Girls Club. Our daughter, though very young, was becoming the best athlete in our family and was an outstanding player on her own little team. Together Tim and I coached a little girls' softball team and loved it. The parents and children of the club were like extended family, and we didn't want to leave them. I loved my church and my Sunday School students, who were also like extended family. I belonged to the Lanham Area Homemakers Club where friendships ran long and deep. Our Homemakers club had socials where our husbands met and established lasting friendships. I didn't want to leave our community, and had it not been for bussing we would have spent the rest of our lives there.

However, our children's education was our top priority, and plans were being made to move to Virginia, as soon as our oldest son graduated from high school. So it was with heavy heart that I asked my "spirit guides" for their advice and they gave it.

I was told that I would move to a **"stone house"** where my **"level would elevate."** I wasn't quite sure what *they* meant by *"elevating my level."* However, *"elevate your level"* was repeated almost every day for many years. Did it mean educational, financial, or spiritual, or all of the above? The term was never explained to me by my spirit friends at that time, but eventually I learned exactly what it meant.

There were also other phrases repeated almost every day: **"Bluebirds will lead you ... ten miles from Reston ... stone house ... riverbend ... move in November."**

When on February 6, 1973, I received a very strange message, it, like many others, made no sense. It read: **"More grief for President, Oval Room will tell ... Oval Room will tell."** What did these words mean? It was true, President Nixon was currently under attack by the *Washington Post* almost every day for something called the Watergate break-in, and February 7 the Senate voted 70-0 to establish a select committee to investigate Watergate. However, when the message, **"Grief for President, Oval Room will tell"** appeared, the investigation had not yet begun and I, like everyone else in the United States, had not begun to comprehend the ramifications of a couple of guys breaking into the Democratic National Committee on June 17, 1972, located in a building called Watergate, would ultimately cause the downfall of the President of the United States. This lay ahead.

For the moment I was more interested in finding or building a new home in Virginia. I was looking forward to a stone house, as my guides were promising, and perhaps one with an oval room.

I spent less and less time doing automatic writing, devoting more and more time to finding a home or a lot on which to build a home. When I did write, so many words and phrases were repeated that my writing was becoming redundant and jaded. **"Bluebirds will lead you ... stone house. move in November ... level will elevate ... ten miles from Reston ... Riverbend ... More grief for President ... Oval room will tell."** I thought about President Nixon and knew that he was in trouble, but how could a room *"tell"* anyone anything? Rooms can't talk. And besides, if it was referring to the President's Oval Office, why didn't they say *office*? I had never heard the Oval Office of the President called "Oval Room."

We spent our weekends looking all over northern Virginia for a home or a lot. Finally, through a friend from childhood, we were introduced to a builder who was opening up a new subdivision in Haymarket, Virginia. It was a little farther away from Washington and Tim's office than we wanted to go, but a full acre of land with a view of Bull Run Mountain made it irresistible.

As soon as we chose our lot, Flora and I drove out to see it and a strange thing happened. Just as we approached our new lot, a bluebird flew right in front of my car at eye level. Flora and I squealed in astonishment. I hadn't seen a bluebird since I was a child visiting my aunt and uncle in southwestern Virginia, and Flora told me it was the first bluebird she had seen in many years.

I knew my guides had led me to the right place, but there were some things that didn't fit. First of all, we were much more than ten miles from Reston, or so I thought. If we were to drive from Reston to my lot it would have been much longer than ten miles, but when I took out a map and measured the distance as the crow flies (or perhaps as the bluebird flies), it was exactly ten miles. The location was also not very far from a street named Riverbend. Now all I needed was to move into my stone house in the month of November to validate the accuracy of my writing. But that didn't happen, at least not with this house. We inquired about having the builder substitute stone for brick and vinyl siding, but the cost was prohibitive. I began to doubt my writing. It's true, I was disappointed that I was unable to have a stone house, but I was even more disappointed that my guides had made a promise or prediction that did not hold true. Again, I was about to give up writing altogether.

We moved temporarily into an apartment and were told that our home would be ready before the school year started in September. In the mean time I drove to the house every other day to check its progress. I also stopped by a hardware store along the way, bought a bluebird house, and was on a ladder nailing it onto a tree by the road when a local farmer drove up and stopped. The friendly farmer asked me what kind of bird I was expecting and I answered, "Bluebirds." He grinned and said, "You ain't gonna get no bluebirds, lady. We had a hard freeze back in the fifties, and we haven't seen a bluebird in these parts since." I told him that I had already seen one just a few weeks ago. He laughed and said it must have been an indigo bunting. I just smiled and continued to secure the bluebird house to the tree. The next time I came to check on the progress of my house I saw a bluebird fly into the bluebird house. Wow, I thought, this is awesome.

On July 13, 1973, as I was zipping along Route 66 on my way to check on the progress of our new home with the radio tuned to the all-news station WAVA, the announcer said, *"Well, I guess there is more grief for the president. It was reported in an interview with the staff of the Senate Committee by Alexander Butterfield that the Oval Room has been secretly recording conversations."* I was so shaken that I had to pull off onto the shoulder of Route 66 to catch my breath. The announcer had used almost the exact words as my writing, including using the term *Oval Room* rather than *Oval Office*. And if conversations in the Oval Room had been tape-recorded it would indeed tell all. The Oval Room did indeed have a voice and was just about to speak. Wow!

Again, it was made clear to me that automatic writing *did not* come from my subconscious mind. If that were true, my subconscious mind would have had to meander around the president's office and check out the listening devices. I wondered if the FBI or Secret Service was aware of all the subconscious minds wandering around in secured buildings gathering information.

WATERGATE IN PROPER PERSPECTIVE

PROGRAM #537

Senator Cal Curtis, Nebraska Republican, says he would not defend the people responsible, or who took part in Watergate, but he believes, as does this reporter, that it has been vastly overplayed and blown out of proportion.

It does not constitute betrayal of our country, nor a pilfering of the treasury; no elected official was involved; and no one died as a result. President Nixon did not invent the wiretap, nor did he plot Watergate. He did not condone it, and the facts were withheld from him too long after it happened.

Said Senator Curtis, addressing the United States Senate, "There were those unable to get Nixon last November, and they're determined to get Nixon now." Senator Curtis makes the following points: "Watergate has brought into being a determined and militant coalition whose object is not justice, but rather—to get Nixon. These include the Nixon haters, a group of politico-sadists of the same type who enjoyed efforts to destroy Lyndon Johnson; a small segment of newsmen who prefer political propaganda over objective reporting; a few extreme partisans whose sense of justice is numbed by their desire for political gain. And finally, those politicians willing to exploit any issue for personal publicity."

Yes, we are a government of law, and stability of the government and ordinary justice demand that the judicial processes, and the rules of evidence, be faithfully followed. Hearsay, rumor, gossip, partial truths, innendos, suspicions, and imaginations buoyed by self-interest, have no place in the American system of justice; and to indulge in such is not in the public interest.

And Senator Curtis continued, as he spoke before the United States Senate, "The offer of immunity to a wrongdoer who has violated the law may place before him a greater temptation than he can bear. The immunity statute has no place in proceedings such as Watergate—and, to dangle before a law violator the promise that he may go scot free, if he involved someone else, can be an obstruction of justice as wrong in its consequences as any conspiracy to obstruct justice, which is perpetrated by actual law violators, themselves.

My friends, what a sad commentary it is that at this moment in history, when President Nixon is so deeply involved in negotiations that may well save the world from nuclear incineration, that he should be distracted for even a fleeting moment by the spectacle of Watergate.

Recently, when I was previleged to visit the President in the Oval Room at the White House, and then to walk alone with him in the Rose Garden, my longtime friend looked at me and said, concerning Watergate, "Call me many things, but don't call me stupid. I am not stupid."

In the words of Senator Carl Curtis, "President Nixon will go down in history as a great and courageous leader, long after all his critics have been forgotten."

How the White House Tapes Came to Light

TAPES, From A1

[illegible]

The White House Tapes

How Ervin's Men Struck Gold

By Jules Witcover
Washington Post Staff Writer

At about 5:30 p.m. on Friday the 13th of July, three men and a woman sat at a conference table in a small interview room of the Senate Watergate committee and learned a secret that could make or break the case against President Nixon.

A fourth man, former White House aide Alexander P. Butterfield, sat with them, as he had for three hours, answering question after question about his role as "executor" of the President's daily schedule.

Butterfield, now federal aviation administrator, was what the Watergate committee staff calls "a satellite witness." He was called in, in a kind of dragnet technique, to discuss in private what he knew as a result of his proximity to major figures in the case. Butterfield's main entree was his

ALEXANDER BUTTERFIELD
. . . held the key

boss, former White House chief of staff H. R. (Bob) Haldeman.

The interrogators were Donald G. Sanders, an assistant minority staff counsel, and staff investigators Scott Armstrong and Gene Boyce. Marianne Brazer, a staff secretary, took notes.

Sanders recalled to Butterfield that former White House counsel John W. Dean III had testified that at the close of a key meeting with President Nixon in the Executive Office Building on April 15, Mr. Nixon had done something strange.

The President, Dean said, had moved off to a corner of the room to say in a "barely audible tone [that] he was probably foolish to have discussed" an offer of executive clemency for Watergate conspirator E. Howard Hunt Jr. with Charles W. Colson, another White House aide.

Could he state to his own knowledge, Sanders now asked Butterfield, whether

See TAPES, A11, Col. 1

Chapter 12

Seagulls Live at the Sea

In retrospect, I believe my move to Haymarket was a stepping-stone. Granted, there were bluebirds, we were located about ten miles from Reston, and there was a street named Riverbend nearby. However, we moved in on December 7, rather than November, and my house was made of brick and vinyl, not stone as I had been promised by my guides.

I met some very nice people in Haymarket, but there was no one with whom I could share my secret and I felt isolated from old friends. Also, telephone calls were toll calls so I tried to keep them reasonably short. To make matters even worse, there was a gas crunch and long drives were frowned upon. I was also beginning to believe my writing was not from a high spiritual source. After all, God is perfect and my writing was not. In the three years I lived in Haymarket I lost interest and rarely did any automatic writing. I went back to work for the Department of Agriculture and resumed my old hobby, oil painting. Tim and I also enjoyed following our daughter's softball games at school and in a community league where she was fast becoming an outstanding athlete. The bad luck of the draw handed my oldest son, Dan, a number 7, and he was drafted during the Viet Nam War. Fortunately, he was not sent overseas. My middle son made friends fast and enjoyed his high school years in Haymarket.

Sometime in March of 1978, Flora called and asked me to do some writing for her. There was something going on in her family and she wanted to see if my guides had advice for her.

When we finished our conversation I sat at the kitchen table, prayed, and put my pen to the paper. To my surprise, the pen moved strong and the writing was clear. The message, however, seemed ridiculous. **"Seagulls live at the sea,"** it wrote. **"Seagulls live at the sea, Seagull visits your child, The Seagull shall set the child free Day of friendship necessary to catch criminal."** Two fancy capital *L's* followed by **"Boo" "L L boo" "Seagulls live at the sea, Sullivan Seagull."** These words and phrases were repeated many times interspersed with unreadable scribble.

"How silly can you get?" I thought aloud. "I'm writing this for Flora and she's from Maine. Even people who are not from Maine know seagulls live at the sea." None of it made any sense, but I called Flora to tell her about the message. She was equally baffled by the words as we tried unsuccessfully to decipher some hidden meaning. I tore the pages from my tablet, folded them, and put them in my purse. I would show the writing to Flora the next time Tim and I went to a Maryland Terrapins' game in College Park. Perhaps there would be something in the scribbles that would make sense to Flora.

In April, I was saddened to learn of the death of a young man from our old neighborhood in Washington and made plans to attend the funeral. There were many old and dear friends from our old neighborhood there, and although it was a sad occasion, it was comforting to be with them again.

As I was about to enter the church I spied my old friend from childhood, the one who had introduced me to my builder, and we sat together. (To respect her privacy, I shall call her Katherine.) Although we had grown up together and had been close friends, we hadn't seen much of each other recently. She lived some distance from me and had a full-time job. I was glad to be with her again. Katherine had gone through some difficult times since we graduated from high school. Her first husband chased women and their marriage had ended in divorce, leaving her with three children to support. She had been married for the second time for about a year and a half, and it was good to see her happy again. I had met her new husband when they stopped by one day to see my new house. Her new husband seemed like a very nice, gentle, and loving man. I especially liked the way he seemed to have made Katherine's children his own and was openly affectionate with them, especially her youngest daughter Amy,* now age nine. We vowed we would try to make time to visit more often.

On the day following the funeral, Katherine called me. She was choking on tears that made it difficult to understand what she was trying to tell me. She asked if I could come to her house as soon as possible. Katherine had not been a person prone to hysterics, and I knew the situation, whatever it was, had to be very serious. Hastily I wrote a note to Tim, grabbed my purse, and jumped into the car. What could possibly upset her so much?

I tried to keep my mind on my driving and resisted breaking the speed limit, but it wasn't easy. Adding to my frustration, the Washington Beltway was crowded with traffic and the drive seemed endless. Katherine was one person with whom I had considered sharing my secret of automatic writing, but had changed my mind, mostly because we had very little one-on-one time together. On the rare occasions when we were together there were always children present and automatic writing is *not* for children.

As I pulled into her driveway, my stomach churned and my knees quivered. I didn't know what was wrong, but my intuition told me that it was bad news. Nothing, however, could have prepared me for the story I was about to hear.

Katherine's eyes were red and swollen; her face was void of color, and her voice trembled as she invited me into her living room. I had never witnessed anguish like this. I almost didn't want to hear what she had to tell me.

She had just discovered that her new husband had been sexually molesting her youngest daughter, Amy, almost from the beginning of their marriage. We both began to cry. Amy was a sweet, trusting child who loved everyone, loved her animals, and loved her mother. That bastard had taken advantage of all those wonderful traits and used them to satisfy his selfish, perverted sexual desires. At that moment I knew I was capable of murder. And if rage ran that strong through me, I could only imagine what Katherine was going through.

It took quite a while for us to gain enough composure for Katherine to tell me all that had transpired the night before.

It seems Katherine and her husband had plans to meet friends for dinner after she returned from the funeral. Her husband, whom I'll call Larry, was in a bad mood and refused to go. Katherine was upset with him and decided to join their friends without him. Her oldest daughter, Leigh, had a dinner date, her son was out with friends, leaving Larry to take care of Amy. Leigh and her boyfriend had decided to go bowling after dinner and she had come home to change clothes. When she entered the house, everything was quiet except for the TV in her mother's bedroom. As she passed the closed door, she stopped and tried to turn the knob, calling for Amy and her mother. The door was locked. She knocked on the door and called Larry's name, then her mother, then Amy. After a considerable amount of time Larry opened the door slightly, and playfully said, "Boo." "Amy and I are watching TV; your mother went out to dinner with her friends." Leigh felt that something wasn't right. Why had Larry locked the bedroom door while he and Amy were watching TV? She asked Amy if everything was okay and Amy answered, "Yes."

Leigh changed her clothes and went to meet her boyfriend to go bowling. Leigh confided to her boyfriend that she had an uneasy feeling when she found her mother's bedroom door locked with Amy and Larry inside. They wondered if something was happening that neither of them wanted to believe.

As soon as Leigh returned home she went straight to Amy's bedroom and asked her if Larry was doing anything bad with her and if he was, she could tell her anything. Amy assured Leigh that nothing bad was happening, and Leigh reluctantly went to her room and tried to sleep.

A short time later, Katherine returned from dinner with her friends, crawled into bed with her husband, and fell asleep.

At about daybreak Amy ran into Leigh's room crying and crawled into bed with her. "The seagull made me tell," she cried. "He's sitting in my window and won't shut up." Half asleep, Amy began to cry even harder and told her sister that Larry had been doing ugly things to her for a long time, but had threatened to kill her cat, her brother, and her sister if she told her mother. He also stressed that her mother might commit suicide if she ever found out what was going on.

Leigh dressed hurriedly, drove to her father's home, and told him the whole story.

In the meantime Katherine had awakened, come downstairs, and was in the process of preparing a big breakfast for the family when the telephone rang. It was her first husband. His voice pleaded, "If you have ever done anything for me in your life, bring Amy with you to my house *NOW*!" Katherine said that the urgency in his voice and knowing that in spite of their divorce, he cared deeply for his children sent her scurrying to the car with little Amy. Amy sat quietly as they drove, her face unreadable, yet she seemed limp and changed in some way.

Upon arriving at the home of her former husband, Amy told the horrible story and it ripped Katherine's heart out. Her beloved husband had been molesting her beloved little girl. At that moment Katherine ripped off her wedding ring and threw it across the room.

Katherine told me that the rest of that evening was a blur; the hospital, the examination of her daughter, the arrest of her husband, the policemen, the questions, and then the final moment of comprehending the truth. A more agonizing truth, I could not imagine any mother having to face.

As we sat on her sofa, Katherine also confided in me that she felt guilty for going out with friends, leaving her daughter in the care of her husband. I reassured her that none of this was her fault. Had she *not* gone out with friends Larry may *not* have been caught and the molestation might still be going on.

Then it hit me! *"Day of friendship necessary to catch criminal."* Oh my God, I thought, my automatic writing in March had not been a message for Flora but a message for Katherine. A seagull had indeed visited her child, had sat on her windowsill in a subdivision far from the sea, and cried out for her to tell her sister. The seagull had indeed *"set the child free."*

I opened my purse and removed the folded paper. "I don't know if this is the right time to tell you this, Katherine, but I do something called automatic writing and this message was written in March." We read the words in amazement. After a time, Katherine said that she was comforted to know that her *"day of friendship"* was *"necessary"* to catch Larry in order to put an end to the molestation of her daughter. We both felt the whole day had been choreographed in another realm of reality, a realm of reality that is anxious to communicate with all of us. We need only to be open to it.

Katherine asked if she could have the paper containing the automatic writing; she wanted to show it to Leigh and I gave it to her. Later, when Leigh saw the paper, she noticed something that I had overlooked among the scribble. The large and fancy *"L L boo."* Leigh said that was the way she made her L's in her initials "L.L." and of course remembered how Larry had opened the bedroom door with a playful "Boo."

It wasn't until almost ten years later, while sitting in a doctor's office, that the final piece of the cryptic message of March 1978 fell into place. I happened to pick up a magazine that contained an article about Jonathan Livingston Seagull and discovered that a character called Sullivan had been Jonathan's spiritual advisor. *"Sullivan Seagull"* was indeed a spiritual advisor, not only to Jonathan Livingston, but also to all of us who are willing to listen. *Sullivan Seagull had set the child free.*

**This story is true. The names, places, and a few details in the chapter were changed for obvious reasons.*

Chapter 13

Stone House and Bluebirds

I have begun to think that Tim in a past life had been a nomad, moving his tent from place to place whenever the pasture looked greener on the other side of the mountain. Tim welcomes change, especially the location of his home, and unlike me, he seems to form no attachment to places. Even though I know change is inevitable, whether I welcome it or fight it, I seem compelled to fight the futile battle. So it was another call to arms when Tim suggested another move. Even though Tim had been right before, all moves we had made had been for our highest good, I dug in my heels.

It was therefore cause for considerable trepidation when my writing also began to tell me of another move. After the seagull had *"set the child free"* just as it had been foretold in my automatic writing, I again trusted my messengers and wrote almost every morning. And almost every morning these words were repeated: **"move, stone house, November, bluebirds, move, level will elevate, oak tree, bluebirds, stone house, bluebirds in oak tree, your level will elevate, move November."**

There were also many messages of encouragement through some challenges in my personal life. I learned through my writing that life was a school and each challenge a learning experience. I came to understand that if I didn't learn my lesson well the first time, the lesson would be repeated, wearing a different face or called by another name. At the top of my paper, before doing my daily writing, I would ask, "What is the most important lesson I need to understand in my life today?" The answer was always the same: *"Elevate Your Level."* The term seemed ambiguous. A person could elevate their level in many areas: educational, financial, emotional, or spiritual. Where did *they* want *me* to start? What did *they* want *me* to do? Should I go back to school, get a job, seek counseling, go back to church or meditate more? *They* didn't, however, elaborate or give me specific instructions; *they* left the figuring out to me.

Tim was now thinking of retiring in a few years, and we needed to make plans and decide where we wanted to spend our senior years. We decided we would like to live farther out in the Virginia countryside on about ten acres. Our sons were no longer living at home, and Cindy was now in middle school. It was our plan to find some property and hold onto it until Tim retired and Cindy finished high school. My writing, however, was encouraging me not to wait. Because of Tim's disinterest in my writing, I did not share the messages encouraging the move. The less he knew that my writing was on his side, the better. However, he got the bug anyway. We found a beautiful piece of property that we both loved. There was a big oak tree in the meadow and bluebirds all over the place. We decided to put our home on the market, and if it sold by July 31, we would jump the gun and move at the end of Cindy's last year in middle school. That way she would be able to begin her high school years in the new location. However, the housing market was depressed for sellers, and everything moved slowly in the late seventies, especially this far away from the city, and gas lines were getting longer. Tim, knowing I would resist the move, asked me if I would like to build a stone house on the property, and he bribed Cindy with the promise of a horse. During our stay in Haymarket Cindy had come to love horseback riding and desperately wanted a horse of her own. I placed the entire situation into God's hands and released it. If our house sold by July 31, it would be God's will that we move; if it didn't, we would stay. I was at peace either way.

To our great surprise, we received a contract on July 20 at the asking price. We would move. Now we had to find a place to live, settle on house plans, and find a contractor and stonemasons, and we hadn't much time. The realtor who sold us our ten acres found a lovely old farmhouse for us to rent while our new house was being built. We weren't aware that rental property in this rural area was almost impossible to come by. But once more things seemed to fall into place as if they were being choreographed from another realm. This seemed to be a lesson I needed to learn: we don't control much of anything; stuff just happens. Our free will comes into play only with our decision on how to handle the "stuff."

We found a builder who came highly recommended from some friends in Haymarket. We went to see their house that was under construction and found the workmanship outstanding. We signed a contract with the builder the same week we moved into the rented farmhouse, September 1, 1978, just in time for Cindy to enter her new high school as a freshman. The following week we went horse shopping, bought the horse, and everyone was happy.

When I asked the builder how long it would take to complete the house, he answered, "Six or seven months." Then I asked, "If Murphy's law should come into play, what is the longest time it could possibly take to move in?" "It could be as long as one year, sometimes stone masons are slow," he answered. I was thinking of two things when I asked that question, the lease on the farmhouse, and what my automatic writing had said about moving in November. If the house were finished in the spring as promised, we would move in March or April. If Murphy was enforcing his law, we might not be able to move in until September. No way could we move in November. But Mr. Murphy applied his law in double doses. Our builder, who was an excellent tradesman, lacked ability when it came to paperwork. He misapplied some of our funds to another house, and we ended up in court. The wonderful stonemason we hired in September had quadruple bypass surgery in November and had to cancel the contract. I checked with other stonemasons but found none to my liking. I didn't even like the type of stone they were bringing me, and their prices were more than we could afford. Again, I acquiesced and decided to have only a small portion of trim in stone.

In June I contacted my old stonemason to see if he would sell us stone from his source. When he asked if I was going to be at home the next day because he wanted to talk to me, I thought it would be to agree upon the price of the stone. I was astonished to learn that when the phone had rung when I called the day before, he had just returned from the doctor who had given this seventy-year-old man permission to go back to work but he hadn't even had time to tell his wife.

We renewed our contract and my stone house became a reality. Exactly as my writing had told me so many years ago, we moved into our stone house on November 1, 1979, and there must have been a dozen bluebirds in our yard that day to help us celebrate.

Chapter 14

Out of the Closet

Living in my stone house at the foot of a small mountain, surrounded by bluebirds, I didn't think life could get any better. I felt a deep gratitude to my spirit guides who had helped me overcome many obstacles and directed me to this little piece of heaven. I thought I had achieved the elevated level of which my guides had written so often and for so long, but I had only just begun. If this book had been written in 1979, I could have left you with the fairy-tale ending, "She moved into her stone house in November, surrounded by bluebirds, and lived happily ever after," but this story is no fairy tale.

Ahead of me would be more than twenty years of elevating my level one step at a time; some steps were very difficult with numerous slips and slides along my path, and other times angels seemed to appear bringing mystical experiences to elevate the level of my consciousness.

On the day we moved into our new home there was an emergency at Tim's workplace that meant many hours of overtime and numerous trips. In addition to the long days on the job was the two-hour drive to D.C. every day and it became too much. Tim moved in with my parents in Annandale, Virginia, during the week, came home each Friday evening, and left before daybreak on Monday mornings. This was not my choice, but it did provide more time to devote to spiritual growth. Tim and I were high school sweethearts and married young. Now with both sons married and living far away, and Cindy in high school, I was for the first time in my life free to plan my day without living on someone else's schedule.

It seems I had been directed to the right place at the right time to meet the right people with time to call my own. I began to get serious about meditation and read many "how-to" books, listened to many guided meditation tapes, and began each day with prayer, meditation, and automatic writing.

In one of the meditation guidebooks, it said to try to visualize a white light, but the light that came to me was a pulsating purple or ultraviolet neon-like light with a golden center. I loved my beautiful purple light. It brought me peace, tranquility, and more energy than I had ever known in my life, but it wasn't that special "white light" of which I had been reading. I thought my meditation had failed or I was somehow unworthy of the white light.

One day I received in the mail a little booklet entitled "Daily Word," a gift from Mildred Morrow, who was now retired and living in Florida. I fell in love with "Daily Word" immediately. I *had* to know more about this philosophy that was so uplifting and positive. It came from a place called Unity Village in Missouri. I *had* to find out if there was a branch of Unity near me. I discovered that there was, and it was located in Charlottesville, Virginia, just about thirty-five miles from me and I *had* to go!

Unity in Charlottesville was between ministers and the service was conducted by members of the congregation in a small room in a shopping center, but there was more spiritual power packed into that tiny room than in any church I had ever attended. The service began with a guided meditation. This was my first experience in a group meditation, and my purple light pulsated with more brilliance than I had ever seen before and I knew I had found my spiritual home.

I happened to sit beside a friendly older lady named Ginny, who asked if I would like to have lunch after church. Tim was on a trip and Cindy had made plans to be with friends so I was free. Our lunch lasted for nearly three hours. She shared with me some of her spiritual experiences to which my automatic writing paled by comparison. Her minister in California was a vocal channel. I knew I could share my secret with her.

Ginny was interested and wanted me to come to her home and give her a demonstration. I don't remember exactly what came out in my writing that day, but I also shared some of the experiences of fulfilled prophecy such as the bluebirds and my stone house, and she shared with me some very interesting spiritual experiences of her life. It was so good to be with someone with whom I could be completely myself. I had been very careful to keep my secret writing to myself for nearly a decade for fear of ridicule.

A few weeks later as we were leaving a Unity Sunday service, Ginny introduced me to a few people and as we stood there in the group Ginny said, "This is Carolyn Daly, she does automatic writing." My knees weakened and my jaw dropped. Ginny was announcing my carefully guarded secret to a group of virtual strangers. I wanted to duck under a chair. I hadn't eased myself out of the closet; I had been shoved out, right in the middle of a group of strangers.

Chapter 15

Unity in Charlottesville

Have you ever had one of those humiliating dreams when you found yourself standing buck naked in a crowd? If you have, you will know exactly how I felt that day at Unity. Of course it was all for the good, there was nothing I needed to hide. My carefully guarded secret didn't raise an eyebrow. There were some in the group who were interested, but no one passed any kind of negative judgment. The people in that group plus many more from Unity in Charlottesville would soon become some of my closest friends.

A small group started meeting at Ginny's home one evening a week to discuss anything of a spiritual nature that we decided was important. I did some writing; Ginny demonstrated the use of a divining rod, not to find water but to find answers. Ginny made a set of divining rods from two old metal coat hangers bent to an "L" shape. I was shocked when I held them in my hand and felt them take on a life of their own. Sometimes the answer was so strong that they actually spun around in my hand. Ginny gave me that set, and I still have them. I used them once to find water on Flora's property. It worked. The well digger found water in the same place. In the 1980s, after Mike retired, Flora and Mike built a home only about twenty minutes away from us. It was wonderful to have her so close again.

Unity hired a new minister, and I was there for his first sermon. A few months later there was a ceremony to welcome new members into Unity in Charlottesville. When the minister said that the only requirement to join Unity was to love God and search for truth, I knew this was the church for me. I joined Unity in Charlottesville the following month. Unlike other churches I had attended, this church not only allowed freedom of thought, they encouraged it. I attended every class that was available and still hungered for more.

Meditation, followed by automatic writing, became a part of my daily routine. I would no more think of missing my meditation time than I would forego brushing my teeth. Most always, I saw on the screen of my mind the beautiful pulsating purple light with a golden center. Then one day came an experience that I shall never forget. I sat in my meditation chair as always, using a headset while listening to a guided meditation. It began as usual with my purple and golden light. Then a small speck of magenta appeared in the middle of the gold. As it grew closer, it took on the appearance of a pulsating human heart, growing ever larger. In the center of the heart appeared the letter "C" in a vibrating blue, outlined in gold and bringing with it a physical sensation of ecstasy that completely enveloped me with the most intense feeling of love I have ever experienced. I wanted to hold onto that moment forever, but it gradually faded away. However, the experience infused me with a vibrant spiritual energy, and I floated on a cloud of joy all day. Nothing in the outside world was able to penetrate my inner peace and exuberant joy. When I had the same experience the following day, I thought that all future meditations would be like the last two, but it never happened again. I yearned and prayed to have that experience again, and when it didn't happen I felt that I had somehow fallen from Grace. Later, my writing told me that my **"experience was a spiritual gift and that gifts were given freely and spontaneously and are not given on demand."**

I described my meditations to my minister and asked him what he thought the letter "C" meant. Did it stand for Carolyn, Christ, or the Christ Consciousness? He answered that he thought it stood for all of those things. Perhaps it was a spiritual baptism.

The experience of this meditation changed me profoundly. I found myself infused with more energy, self-confidence, and better health than I had ever known even in my youth. It was a life without fatigue or illness; I could accomplish more in one day than I ever thought possible; I was able to know and understand things that I had never been taught; my automatic writing became clearer and the messages more beautiful. Then one day a message came from my automatic writing that said: **"Joy is spiritual energy and cannot be depleted. When your work is a joy, it is no longer work; it is play."**

What a wonderful truth that is. Haven't we all had all the energy we needed when we were doing something that was pure joy?

I became very active in Unity in Charlottesville. I was elected to the board of directors and served a term as president.

The mysterious writings of long ago had come to pass and I understood what it meant to *"Elevate my Level."* But I wanted to continue to *"Elevate my Level"* and signed up for every available class offered by Unity and other groups. Learning was now my joy, and I never tired of it. I studied books written about and by Charles and Myrtle Fillmore, founders of Unity; books by Lao and Walter Russell, *Therapeutic Touch; Attitudinal Healing* by Susan Trout; to mention only a few. However, it was *A Course in Miracles* that would once again *"Elevate my Level"* bringing with it a new meaning to the term automatic writing.

Chapter 16

A Course in Miracles and the Coming of the Cosmos

When I was first invited to join a class to study a book entitled *A Course in Miracles,* I wasn't sure it was for me. I wondered if the class was taking instruction in how to turn water to wine, raise the dead, or walk on water. However, my friend Ginny persuaded me to give it a try just once, and I reluctantly agreed.

The group met in a doctor's office after hours. They were just given a key and allowed to use it. How trusting, I thought.

The night we came for the first time there was only one other person there with Ginny and me. As we waited for others I glanced through the book, *A Course in Miracles,* and happened to open to a passage that said: *"Sin is defined as 'lack of love.' Since love is all there is, sin, in the sight of the Holy Spirit is a mistake to be corrected, rather than an evil to be punished."* This definition of *sin* appealed to me. For my whole life I was taught that I was born in sin and remained in unforgiven sin until I accepted Jesus as my Savior. To me this meant that the whole world was born in sin, and all who never had the opportunity to know Jesus were condemned to Hell, regardless of the kind of life they lead. Even as a small child, I felt this was unfair. I was also taught that God is Love. Would a loving God send little babies to Hell just because they were born in sin and never had an opportunity to accept Jesus? Would a God of love send all people of other faiths to Hell, even when they had lived an exemplary life and had died without ever hearing the name Jesus? Of course we all have sinned, but sin defined as a mistake to be corrected rather than an evil to be punished seemed much more logical coming from a loving God. That sentence was a grabber. And so began my study of *A Course in Miracles (ACIM).* Even the first time I read some of the passages, they seemed strangely familiar to me, for many of the messages were the same messages I had received from my writing over the years. The wording was not exactly the same, but there was no doubt about the meaning. I also found it interesting that I began to do automatic writing at about the same time as *ACIM* was being received and written in New York City.

From my first *ACIM* study group there emerged a smaller group that formed a Foundation for the Study and Application of *A Course in Miracles* and I was an active participant. FSACIM held workshops dealing with various principles of *ACIM*. Since the *Course* itself was written via spiritual dictation from Jesus through a Jewish lady doctor, my automatic writing was also offered as a workshop.

My first workshop on automatic writing.

Mayhurst, Orange, Virginia, July 1992.

I shall always remember that first workshop. The number of people who signed up for it astounded me, more than twenty. It had been twenty years since I began to write, and for seventeen of those years I had kept it secret. Now here I stand in front of a room-full of people sharing my experience and offering them the opportunity to try automatic writing in a safe and loving place. I thought, "Carolyn, you've come a long way since those first frightening attempts to do automatic writing back in April of 1972."

My second workshop was held at Swannanoa, on Afton Mountain, the home of Walter and Lao Russell. I couldn't believe that *I* was standing behind a lectern on that marvelous marble stairway, giving a workshop on automatic writing to a large and interested audience.

Swannanoa held a special place in my heart from the first time I visited there with my cousin in 1987. I vividly recalled my first visit.

My cousin had invited me to visit their campsite at Sherando Lake in August where we had planned to swim, hike, and have a cookout. The day turned out to be unseasonably cold and misty so we had to find something else to do. We had heard something about a castle on nearby Afton Mountain called Swannanoa, where an artist named Walter Russell had a small art gallery. We had also heard that his strange elderly widow still lived there. I was doing well with my art restoration business and taking art lessons at the time, so visiting the gallery of the artist who was commissioned by President Franklin Roosevelt to sculpt the Four Freedoms appealed to me.

Swannanoa

My first glimpse of the white marble castle on the top of Afton Mountain left me breathless. Yes, it was beautiful, but there was something more, something I could only sense, something special, something spiritual.

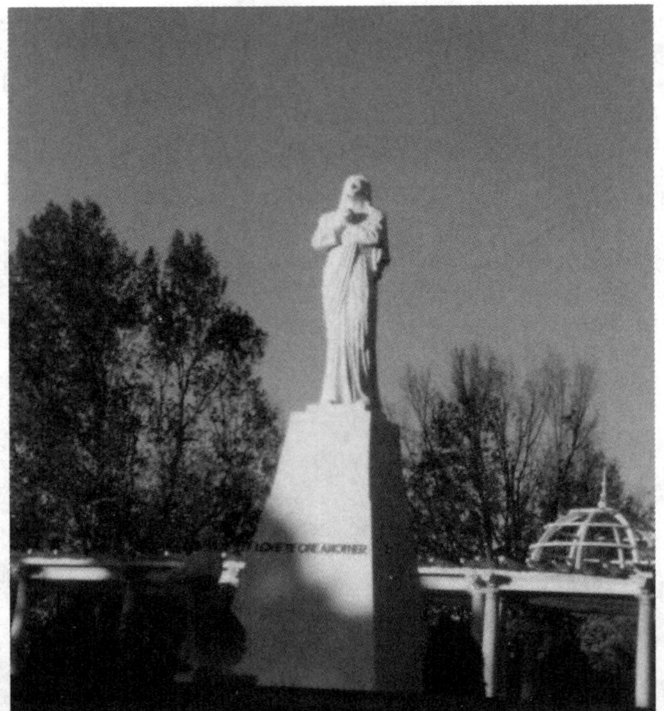

Love Ye One Another

A petite red-haired young lady named Margaret greeted us, told us there was a tour in progress, and asked us to wait. She also told us to feel free to go around back and walk in the garden until the next tour began. As we entered the garden we looked up to see an enormous statue of Christ that watched over all who entered. Inscribed under the statue was: *"Love Ye One Another."* Once more a feeling came over me; it was like meditating with my eyes open.

We walked slowly up a marble staircase admiring a variety of beautiful flowers growing in the garden. When it comes to flowers, I must confess to being botanically challenged, so when we noticed a beautiful bright pink flower growing from a crack in the marble wall, I hadn't the foggiest idea what it was called. I only knew that I admired its ability to overcome the adversity of where its little seed had landed and grow to be even more beautiful than its sisters and brothers who were growing in the well-tended garden.

In art class I was going to begin watercolor for the first time. It wasn't that I thought this little flower would make a lovely watercolor painting; it was that *I knew I had to paint it.* Without a camera or sketchpad I tried to etch the little flower and its surroundings in my mind.

At last we were then invited inside Swannanoa for our tour. Stepping through the doorway, I looked to see a beautiful marble staircase leading to a landing with an enormous Tiffany stained-glass window glowing from the sunlight behind it. It was magnificent. I couldn't believe that this was really someone's home, that there were people who actually lived in such splendor. In my wildest dreams I could never have imagined that I would one day stand on that very staircase to give a workshop on automatic writing. That day I only knew that there was something special about this day, being at this special place and finding the little flower growing to its fullest potential between a rock and a hard place.

The artwork by Walter and Lao Russell was beautiful, but that wasn't what left the lasting impression of that day. I remembered best the little flower that spoke to my heart and said, *"Paint me."*

Upon returning home, I pulled out my sketchpad and tried to draw the little flower. What kind of flower was it and how many petals did it have? How many steps were on the stairway? I couldn't remember anything so I decided to go back, this time with my camera.

Several days later I returned to Swannanoa and again spoke to Margaret and asked if I could go back to the garden and take a photo of the little flower growing from the marble wall. She readily agreed and told me that the flower I loved so much was a cosmos.

I went to the place where once the flower bloomed to find that it was gone, only the stem remained. I took the photo anyway in order to have the proper background. I had the film developed immediately and was disappointed that although the rest of the roll had turned out perfectly, the four shots of the marble wall were blank.

When my attempt to draw from memory failed, I decided to look up "cosmos" in the dictionary to see if there might be a picture. I at least might find out how many petals it had. I opened Webster's New Collegiate Dictionary (printed in 1953) and found the word "cosmos": (cos'mos [koz'mos] fr. Gr. Kosmos, order and harmony in the world) 1. The universe conceived as an orderly and harmonious system. 2. Hence, order; harmony. 3. Any self-inclusive system characterized by order and harmony. 4. Bot. A tall garden herb of a genus (Cosmos) of the aster family, having fall blooming flowers of various colors.

How appropriate, I thought, my little flower growing between marble slabs meant peace and harmony in the universe. When I looked in a garden book I found a picture of an eight-petaled flower called the cosmos. The shock came when I began to draw it. It almost drew itself, for it was the same little flower which had appeared in my writing from the very first day and had appeared on almost every page of automatic writing I had ever done. I realized immediately that going to Swannanoa on that cold, rainy day in August was not by chance and finding my cosmos growing from a crack in a marble wall was no coincidence.

I returned to Swannanoa again one evening with my camera loaded. Margaret had invited me to come to the garden any time to paint or sketch; the Russells encouraged art. That day turned out to be extra special. I saw Lao Russell walking a pair of black scotch terriers in the garden and wondered if they were descended from President Roosevelt's beloved Scottie, Falla. I didn't want to intrude on Mrs. Russell's privacy so I smiled and went about taking my photos. She came over to me and asked sweetly what I was doing and I told her the whole story of my visits. She embraced me and told me to make myself at home and when my painting was finished, she would like for me to bring it for her to see. She also told me she felt she had known me before and I felt the same about her. It seemed odd to me to think someone had described her as strange. Perhaps the strangeness is in the eye of the beholder.

When I finished the watercolor of the cosmos, I brought it to Swannanoa for Lao Russell to see, even though I felt a little embarrassed to show my first attempt at watercolor to such a world-renowned artist. To my surprise and delight, she liked it so much she asked if I could make a copy for her. I not only made a copy for Mrs. Russell, I made many copies. The painting has come to symbolize the triumph of spirit over adversity and the signature of my precious spirit guide,

Cosmos. I have used the prints for "get well" cards, and it seems to have a special healing quality. Many who were not expected to survive recovered completely. One friend kept it at her bedside in the hospital when she was in critical condition and doctors didn't give her much of a chance to survive. But she did survive and lived ten more wonderful years. She framed the cosmos card and displayed it in her living room. To her it became the symbol of her own recovery.

Lao Russell died before I gave my workshop on the marble staircase of Swannanoa, but I felt her spirit was with me giving me courage to speak before a large audience. I don't know how many of those who attended my workshops have continued their writing, but I know from some of the messages they received that day, they were off to a great start.

OPENING TO FULLNESS OF SPIRIT

Overcoming the Challenges of Life

Chapter 17

Pineapples and Opening to the Fullness of Spirit

Each study group I joined brought me not only more insight into my quest for Truth, but opened my mind to a myriad of possibilities I had never considered. One such class was therapeutic touch that I considered an experiment. I had heard pros and cons on whether or not it was a valid healing treatment, and of course I had to find out for myself. Had I walked into that class ten or fifteen years ago, I would have laughed and walked away.

In a way the term therapeutic touch is a misnomer; no one actually touches anyone. It wasn't like some TV evangelists who lay their hands on someone in a wheelchair, calls out to God, and the person instantly jumps up and starts to dance. Briefly, the person who is to receive the treatment sits in a straight-back chair while two people who administer therapeutic touch stand in front and back. Keeping their hands about two inches from the body, they start at the top of the head and work down to the end of the toes, as if stroking a cat, keeping the motion always in the same direction. Then they switch positions and repeat the procedure. When the givers finish they confer to see if either of them noticed a place on the body that felt either warmer or cooler than the rest of the body. When I first witnessed it, I didn't really believe that the human hand could work as an MRI, scanning the body to locate problem areas, and I certainly didn't believe it would work for me. However, I gave it a try with an open mind and guess what? It worked. I was first a recipient and had told no one that I had been having leg cramps. Both ladies who scanned my body came up with a "hot spot" on the calf of my leg. However, the most beneficial thing to me was how relaxed I felt when the treatment had finished; it was like coming out of a deep meditation. When I became the "giver" and my partner and I both found a "hot spot" in the shoulder area of the recipient, I must admit that I was surprised again. I could actually feel the temperature change in the palms of my hands.

A young lady, who was staying with Tim and me at the time, while finishing her thesis for the University of Virginia, was taking the course with me. (She was also the one who went with me to be regressed in Virginia Beach, where I learned more about my past life as Ellen.)

When we arrived home that night we found Tim very uptight. He had spent the day at the golf course sitting around drinking far too much coffee after the match and couldn't calm down enough to sleep. My friend and I sat him in a chair and told him we were going to use him as a guinea pig to practice what we had learned in therapeutic touch class. Tim reluctantly sat in the chair certain that we had lost our minds, but condescended to humor us. When we finished the procedure Tim could hardly stay awake long enough to find his way to bed.

The following day Tim was stung by a bee on the arch of his bare foot and screamed out in pain. I wasn't sure if therapeutic touch would work with only one person, but I persuaded Tim to let me try. With his bare foot in my lap I used both hands parallel to his foot at about two inches away from the skin. At the point my hand was directly over the bee sting I felt something that was like a pseudo bee sting. That shocked me. I was expecting to feel no more than a warm spot. Almost instantly the pain was gone and the swelling started to subside. Tim, the skeptic, could not deny that therapeutic touch had worked. This doesn't mean that therapeutic touch is a cure all and can heal cancer, but it does mean that there is a strong healing energy that comes through the hands of the healer into the body of the recipient. I can't explain how or why it happens, but I know from my own experience that it does happen.

But healing with therapeutic touch was not my only gain from this class. I met two people there whom I would soon count among my closest friends, Mary and Nancy. Mary had been a Catholic nun for seventeen years before she left the convent and married. Nancy is a bubbly young lady who had heard that I did automatic writing and wanted to learn. Even at our first meeting in the therapeutic touch class, I felt an instant connection, as if I had known these two all my life, and the feeling was mutual. I invited Nancy to my home for a one-on-one class in automatic writing. After prayer and meditation, Nancy was taking her infant steps that would ultimately lead her to do psychic readings. But that is Nancy's journey and her story to tell. One day Nancy, Mary, and I drove to Virginia Beach so Nancy could be regressed by the same person who had regressed me. It was this trip that planted the first seeds that would grow into a group of Pineapples.

It was getting close to Christmas when our group of four, Nancy, Mary, Harriet (a friend from Unity), and I, decided to meet at a restaurant in Charlottesville for lunch. Mary brought with her a friend whom I had not yet met. Her name was Shirley, and she was another of those special people with whom I felt an instant bond. The conversation bubbled like a wellspring with fascinating ideas, theories, and personal experiences. A luncheon that began about 11:15 a.m. lasted until they kicked us out some time after 4:00 p.m. We were shocked when the waitress reminded us of the time.

I had purchased as a Christmas gift for Nancy, Harriet, and Mary a pendant in the shape of a pineapple to symbolize our friendship. My friends asked me if I had bought a matching pineapple necklace for myself and of course I hadn't. Two days later the UPS man pulled into my driveway and delivered to me a pineapple pendant matching the ones I had given them. A little later we bought one for Shirley and so began the Pineapples.

The Pineapples

I had worked with Nancy privately several times on automatic writing and the rest also learned. We would meet from time to time, sit around a table, do our writing, and compare notes. The messages that came from that group were always inspirational and moving. The Pineapples soon grew in numbers and closeness. I always looked forward to our meetings. We not only shared our deepest religious and philosophical theories, but we had lots of laughs.

From time to time some of us still meet, but for many of us, life has taken us in different directions. Sadly, our beloved Mary developed cancer and passed over to the spirit world. However, I feel her loving presence is with us whenever a couple of Pineapples get together.

It was the Pineapple group, together with some students of *A Course in Miracles*, who began to study Susan Trout's book *Attitudinal Healing*. Some of the group took a class in Washington and brought it back to the rest of us. I signed up for the first class, and another group of very intimate friends came into my life.

The course in *Attitudinal Healing* was most beneficial to me in dealing with my relationship with my mother. Like many mother-daughter relationships, my relationship with my mother was stormy. Mother seemed always to be angry, and I never understood why. I tried to please her, but I always failed. One of the exercises Susan Trout taught us was the use of dreams as a healing process. I asked for a dream that would help to heal my relationship with my mother. I thought I had followed the procedure for programming my dream perfectly. However, upon awakening the following morning I thought I had failed. My dream wasn't about my mother, but about a lady that I scarcely knew named Louette.

I was asked to tell my dream in class the next day and so I did. It was as follows:

Louette had asked me to help her find a used car. I told her that I knew nothing about cars and declined. Louette persisted until I finally agreed. I found myself in a place that looked more like the Sanford and Son junkyard than a used-car dealership. As Louette and I wandered through the junk, she said, "Carolyn, look, I think I'll buy this one." She pointed to a rusted-out piece of junk that had no wheels but the price was cheap. Close by was another car that was bright and shiny with a good set of wheels and appeared to have a good engine.

I said, "Why don't you buy this one? At least it has wheels, appears to be in good condition, and the price is only slightly higher." "No," she said stubbornly, "I'm going to buy the cheaper one." I told her that the cost to repair the junk car would be more than the difference in price but she wouldn't listen. "Okay," I said, "if you buy the junk don't expect me to help you take care of the repairs."

The class agreed that Louette was a "stand-in" for my mother and I had released myself from the responsibility for my mother's happiness or unhappiness.

That healing dream lifted an enormous weight from my soul and prepared me for things to come. Yes, I would continue to help Mother as much as possible, but no more would I feel responsible for her unhappiness. She had made her own choices and living with the result of those choices was her responsibility.

Some other friends from Unity established a prayer group that met once a week. It was called "Master Minding." I didn't like the name but I liked the twelve steps in the statement that preceded our prayer requests. With a few modifications of the wording to better suit our objectives, we would read our version of the steps together and then ask God for what we wanted most. I really didn't want "stuff" to add to the material things in my life, so in addition to praying for the sick and unhappy, I asked my spirit guides what I should pray for. Their answer was **"Fullness of Spirit."** That was the first time I had heard that term and didn't quite know what it meant. My spirit guides told me through my automatic writing to pray *only for the fullness of spirit* for myself and others and all that was needed would be given. And so it was from that day until this, the words *Fullness of Spirit* appear on almost every page of my automatic writing. I can't say even now that I fully understand it. I can say that asking for *"Fullness of Spirit"* in prayer brings miracles. Try it for yourself and you will witness amazing results.

My writing also seemed to be harping on "music." Now if I considered myself botanically challenged, when it came to music I was functionally illiterate. When I was a young teenager in my old Baptist church they were trying to establish a junior choir. Under pressure I joined. In the middle of the first practice the minister came over to me and told me that he wanted me to remain in the choir for "window dressing" but asked that I only mouth the words. I was crushed that my singing was that bad and deliberately avoided even singing aloud with the congregation and continued to only mouth the words. Now my guides were encouraging me to do something with music. I chuckled whenever music was mentioned. However, there was a major change in my music preference. Gradually I wanted only to listen to classical music. Most of the time I didn't know the composer or the name of the piece, I only knew I could become lost in the beauty of its sound.

Then came the night when I was in enormous emotional pain and couldn't sleep. I decided to write to see if my spirit guides could give me some information that would relieve my anxiety. As I wrote, I heard a little chant-like melody in my head. The words were few and the melody simple. This is what was written:

Where grows the seed of Eternal Love?

Where is that Sacred Place?

The Giver is the Receiver of Eternal Love

Which is a Gift of God's Grace

God plants the seed of Eternal Love

It grows within you wherever you Grow

Again, I recognize that this is not a Mozart concerto, but I know it did not come *from* me but *through* me and brought me comfort in a time of deep distress.

I went to a musician friend, picked out the melody on a keyboard with one finger, and she put the music onto paper. Later, I was flattered when a man in my Attitudinal Healing class, who majored in music, asked if he could polish up the score and use it in a church service. To say the least, I was deeply honored to think the little chant-like song that had come through me would be used in a church service in another community. I was becoming aware that through automatic writing all things are possible. It brings the wisdom and creativity of the universe to your fingertips and is as limitless as the cosmos. Perhaps knowing and accepting this Truth opens our consciousness to the *Fullness of Spirit*.

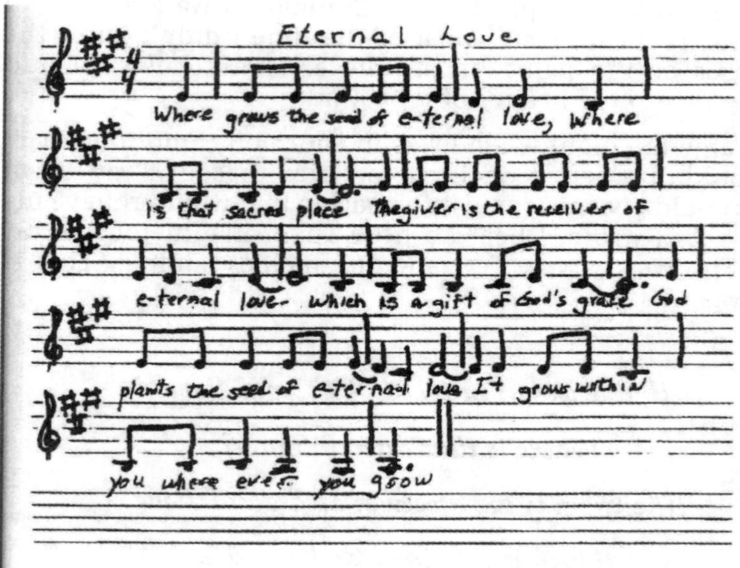

Chapter 18

Pruning

In early March of 1995, I opened my notebook after my meditation and prayer and began to write: *"It will soon be spring, a time for new growth, the flowering of fruit trees whose blossoms will bring forth fruit in their season. But now is the time for pruning. Pruning is painful but necessary. Dead wood must be removed to make way for new growth. Even growth that appears healthy must sometimes be cut away if the tree is to develop to its fullest potential. As it is in the nature of a fruit tree, so it is with my beloved children. Some pruning is done when we recognize those things that hamper our spiritual growth and deliberately remove them from our consciousness. Some pruning is done by the storms of nature. It is this pruning which is least understood and most painful. But know, my child, that pruning, no matter how painful, is necessary to bring forth the blossoms and flowers of springtime for the harvest of sweet fruit in the fullness of spirit, in the fullness of time."*

As I read this message I thought of all the misconceptions and false beliefs I had pruned from my consciousness since that Easter Sunday in 1971, making room for a more open-minded search for Truth. Whenever I recognized the ugly faces of jealousy, greed, fear, prejudice, hurt feelings, or condemnation of others, I would ask God to cleanse them from my consciousness and allow forgiveness of myself and others to take their place. I was satisfied that my pruning was complete, that I was ready to burst forth into full bloom, into the Fullness of Spirit and bring forth sweet fruit. I was wrong.

Storms of nature were brewing just over the horizon, coming to prune away things I loved and prepare me for growth in a new direction. Fortunately the Truths I had learned from my classes, friends I had made along the way, and the messages I received from my beloved spirit guides would sustain me with the knowledge that all things work together for the good and I was being pruned for a higher purpose.

My art restoration business was going great. I had just delivered a group of restored paintings to a favorite customer in Loudoun County, and he had given me five more. I loved the paintings I restored and the challenge of bringing back to life works of art that had come to me looking like my grandmother's dishrag. It was more than the money I received for my work that brought me satisfaction; it was the sometimes teary expressions of appreciation when a family treasure, thought lost forever in disrepair, was transformed to its original beauty. Yes, I had the perfect profession. It was something I would have done for the sheer joy of it even if there were no money involved. As my spirit guides wrote so many times **"Joy is spiritual energy and cannot be depleted."** I could work long hours on restoration and be quite surprised that it was 2:00 a.m. and there was no fatigue.

I had completed four of the five paintings for my customer in Loudoun County when I noticed that my vision just didn't seem quite right. I put an index card over my right eye and I could see normally, but when I put the card over my left eye there seemed to be a dark spot in the center of my field of vision. "It has to be eye strain," I thought, "restoration requires close and precision work and I have been working long hours lately. I'll relax and meditate and it will go away." But it didn't.

When I told Tim about the problem, he told me to call an eye doctor immediately. Because for most of my life, my vision had been 20-20 and I only used drugstore glasses while reading or doing close work, I didn't have an eye doctor. However, there was an ophthalmologist in my Attitudinal Healing class who had become a friend. When I called and told him the problem, he told me to get myself to his office as quickly as possible. I knew from the tone in his voice that this could be serious. It was. He was certain that I had developed a hole in the macular part of the retina. This was confirmed by additional tests at the University of Virginia Hospital, and I was scheduled for immediate surgery in the early morning of April 1, 1995.

The surgeon told me there was an 80 percent chance that the operation would restore my vision. I had no doubt that with God's help, I would be one of the eighty out of one hundred and would be back to restoring paintings, reading, and enjoying all the other things one takes for granted when their vision is near perfect. Besides, I had so many people praying for me, how could the outcome be anything less than perfect?

In midmorning a few hours after the surgery, I had one of the most amazing experiences of my life. Enough time had passed that I was not under the influence of drugs; I was in fact dressed and ready to leave the hospital.

With the type of surgery I had, I was told I must keep my chin on my chest anytime I was in an upright position for the next four weeks and was to sleep on my stomach. As it was more comfortable to lie down than to sit up, I was lying on my stomach but wide awake in the hospital bed. Nurses were scurrying about tending to my roommate who was experiencing loud and foul-smelling indigestion. I turned my head away from my roommate and tried to relax when suddenly my mind seemed to separate from my body. I could see with my eyes closed the most amazing sites with a clarity of vision that I had never experienced with my eyes open. It was as if I had two sets of eyes, one focused on the physical world and the other on an entirely different place. I was spontaneously propelled on a wild and wonderful trip into another realm of existence.

I first saw the stars and planets whizzing by until we came upon another land. I could look below and see ancient villages with grass roofs and tiny people going about their normal lives. I wanted to stop for a closer look, but I had no control over where I was going or what I was seeing; it was all happening at an enormous speed. I noticed below me what appeared to be human beings bogged down and flailing about in something resembling quicksand, struggling to free themselves. I wanted to go down to help, but I wasn't allowed to go closer and had the feeling that they were there for a purpose and it wasn't my job to rescue them. Surprisingly, I felt at peace about that. The next second I was looking across an abyss to a beautiful white city with golden domes. Its splendor was breathtaking and similar to a recurring dream I had from time to time. I definitely wanted to get a closer look at this place and linger a while; however, someone else was in charge of my tour and I had only a brief and distant glimpse. The whole time I was on the trip, I was still aware of the goings-on in my room. A nurse asked me a question, and I pretended to be asleep because I wanted no interruptions. Part of me was also aware of the intestinal problems of my roommate and hoped she'd get over it soon, not so much to ease her pain but because I was annoyed with all the commotion. I selfishly wanted the room to be quiet so I could continue my trip. I was in two places at the same time, and I much preferred the one in outer space. I was enthralled by the experience. The extreme clarity of the vivid colors and sights of my internal vision told me that when my healing process was over, I would be able to see better than ever.

Then, as suddenly as it started it came to an end and the screen of my spiritual vision turned off. I tried to bring it back, but to no avail. Whatever happened to me was completely spontaneous and out of my control, but I enjoyed every moment of it.

In a few minutes Tim came in to take me home. When I told Tim about the experience he passed it off as a hangover from the anesthesia or that I had fallen asleep and I was having one of my weird dreams. I didn't argue, but I knew this experience was no dream. I had been fully conscious and aware of everything going on in the room. I wondered if it was a spontaneous OBE (out of body experience). I had heard of such things when I visited the Monroe Institute some years before. I didn't disbelieve it was possible, but I didn't think it could happen to me. I finally chalked up the experience to a hallucination. Until ...

A few months later I told my Pineapple friends about the experience, and to my surprise my friend Mary told me she had taken the same trip. As we compared notes we discovered that we had seen virtually the same sights. It had also happened to her in the hospital, and she was also annoyed when nurses came in to ask questions. She said she also felt she was in two places at the same time. If we were hallucinating, our minds had taken us on the same adventure to the same place.

My recovery time seemed long. Try walking around with your chin on your chest for even an hour and you'll know how difficult it would be to not be able hold your head in an upright position for a month. My only relief came when a friend from my Attitudinal Healing class brought her massage table over and gave me a wonderful back rub with my face in the hole in the table.

My friends were wonderful. Friends from our golf club provided food every night. A friend who worked at the library brought me books on tape; my friends from my classes in

Charlottesville provided me with tapes from Deepak Chopra; *A Course in Miracles* guided meditations and classical music. When your vision is pruned away, you learn to listen.

When my healing time was finally over and I went in for an eye examination I was shocked. I couldn't even see the entire big "E" on the eye chart. The doctor told me that it takes longer for some to regain their vision than it does for others. Weeks later I was able to see almost the entire big "E" but not much more. To make matters worse, the trauma of the operation caused a cataract to develop. I reached the point that I was legally blind in my right eye. This changed my life. Not only did I have to give up the profession I loved, I couldn't read for more than a few minutes before my left eye would begin to water so much I'd have to quit. This pretty well ended class study. I could drive only in the daylight hours and only when the weather was perfect. If even a little shower came up while I was driving I felt I was a menace to others on the road. I tried to play golf but my depth perception was off so much that I whiffed the ball more often than I hit it. Fortunately, my friends at the golf course were patient, and golf, as bad as it was, seemed to be my only pleasure.

It was also at this time that my mother began to show symptoms of Alzheimer's disease. My sister had to endure most of the problems alone because she lived closer and Mother didn't like to call me because it was a toll call. Mother was frugal. She called my sister as one would call 911. Sometimes she would leave a message on my sister's answering machine, saying in a harsh tone, "This is your mother. Get over here right away and take me to the grocery store, I'm out of buttermilk."

It soon became apparent that Mother would have to go to an assisted living facility. My sister, Addy, and I had not seen a lot of each other after we grew up. I am almost ten years older, and we live almost one hundred miles apart. Mother's illness brought us together, and we became a pretty good team. Our first cousin, Judi, volunteered her help, and soon we became a trio. Judi was like having another sister and could do more with Mother than Addy and I. Mother seemed always to be angry at Addy and me, and no matter what we did to make life better for her it was never enough and never right. And that wasn't the Alzheimer's talking, it had always been that way. However, now it didn't upset me as much. I knew that her unhappiness was more from within herself, and there was nothing my sister or I could do that would change that. She had "bought the junk car and it was her responsibility to repair it."

As time passed and Alzheimer's made further inroads into my mother's brain, she seemed to forget why she didn't like her daughters. Sometimes she would even say "thank you" for things we brought her instead of telling us that it was not what she wanted. She seemed happier to see us when we came and sadder to see us leave. We visited several times a week, and on Thursdays Judi, Addy, and I would take Mother to the Cracker Barrel for lunch. Mother loved the old-fashioned decor and the food. She always topped off her meal with a strawberry sundae. Mother had false teeth so we would always order "a strawberry sundae, without nuts," and Mother would give us a disgusted look and say, "Everybody knows strawberries don't have nuts."

My mother was quite a unique and funny little character. She was only 4'10" with dark eyes, which seemed even darker when she was angry. But now the eyes seemed more mellow, and the fighting spirit had faded away somewhere in the brain where Alzheimer's lives.

Many times throughout her life she would innocently say things that would crack us up. She was so well known for saying something off the wall that when a distant cousin was told that she had Alzheimer's, he remarked, "How would anyone know?"

As long as I'm on the subject I'll tell you some of the embarrassing stories. My friend, Flora, has told me many times that I should write them down for posterity.

When I was in early grade school my parents took me with them to pick out a Christmas tree. We always went to the same Native American who had a stand in the Florida Avenue Market in Washington, D.C. As soon as we arrived, White Feather came over to greet us. "Mrs. Greer," he said, "I have just the tree for you," and held up the tree for us to examine. "No, White Feather," my mother exclaimed, "that's just like the tree you sold us last year and two days after Christmas it looked like a skeleton with balls hanging on it." With that my dad doubled over with laughter. White Feather quickly disappeared into the trees, and Mother gave my father a hefty elbow to the gut and told him to "shut up." My father loved to tell that story on Mother. However, it was many years before I understood the humor.

Another episode occurred on a day Mother had just returned home after spending the summer at their beach place. I was there with my new baby, helping Mother clean her Annandale house when the Fuller Brush man came to the front door and asked if there was anything she needed. "No," she said, "I don't think so." When the salesman was halfway across the yard, she called out, "Oh, do you have anything that would make my drawers smell better?" When I laughed and the salesman blushed, it suddenly registered with Mother that she had said something wrong and she tried to correct herself. "Oh, you know what I mean, my drawers haven't been opened all summer and you know how musty that smells." The salesman ran to his car.

The most recent embarrassment involved a trip to the doctor's office with my sister Addy. The waiting room was crowded when Mother said in a very loud voice, "I need a fan for my vagina." A hush fell over the room as people raised a startled eye over their magazines to see who had made that statement. I'm sure it seemed a curious request coming from a woman in her eighties. My sister hid her blushing face in her magazine and pretended not to notice. Realizing that she had probably misspoke, Mother said, "Vagina, Rigana, Regina, oh, you know, my vacuum cleaner."

As Mother's Alzheimer's grew worse, my relationship with Addy and Judi became closer. My spiritual quest would have been put on hold indefinitely were it not for the curiosity and encouragement from Addy and Judi. After Tim's retirement, I rarely had the alone time to meditate and write, and I was gradually getting out of the habit. But Addy and Judi were not about to allow me to backslide. They felt that I had a special gift and should use it. I told them that anyone could do automatic writing with proper instruction. But they were unconvinced. They had no idea of what spirit had in store for them and neither did I.

In retrospect, I can see more clearly that without pruning, my time would be filled with all the activities I enjoyed most; my restoration business, my classes at Unity, my art classes and painting. These, along with golf, happily consumed a great deal of my time. With my loss of vision this part of my life was pruned away affording me time and desire to put down in writing the story of my spiritual life to share with others who might benefit from my experiences. I now feel my mission in this life was to search for truth and write this book about that search. In retrospect, I can also see that the events that kept Tim working long hours at the office was a pruning of sorts. He moved in with my parents who lived closer to his work, and thus he was able to come home only on weekends, leaving me the time and freedom to grow spiritually and develop my art skills.

Eventually the cataract was removed from my right eye, and my vision improved somewhat so that I was later able to return to all the activities I loved, albeit to a lesser degree. Had it not been for the pruning, this book may never have been written. Writing this book brought me more pleasure than all the things that were pruned away. I am therefore grateful for the pruning.

However, there has also been some pruning done that ripped my heart out and that to this day I don't understand. Perhaps someday I'll know the answers, but for now I can only say the situation is in God's hands. I must release it and have faith that this pruning may be for the benefit of someone else and so I can only let go and let God.

Chapter 19

The Ghost of Terrace Cottage

In September 1998, my daughter Cindy, now living near Detroit, Michigan, invited me to take a Labor Day holiday trip with her and a friend to Mackinac Island, a unique place to vacation where no motorized vehicles are allowed. The three of us loaded bicycles onto Cindy's van and headed north to St. Igness where we boarded a ferry to cross Lake Heron to Mackinac Island.

I would be turning sixty-five in a few days, and bicycles had changed a lot since I last pedaled my bike around my neighborhood in Washington, D.C. To confuse the issue even more, they put the brakes in the wrong place. Everyone my age knows that in order to bring your bike to a halt, you pedal backward. After two trips over the handlebars I finally learned to squeeze the hand brake gently instead of frantically backpedaling. After I finally got the hang of it, I was able to keep up with Cindy, and we managed to bike around the nearly nine-mile shoreline of Mackinac Island, taking in and enjoying all the natural beauty.

When I woke the next morning I expected to be sore from head to toe, but other than two skinned knees and skinned palms from my trips over the handlebars, I felt great. However, we decided that since we would be sightseeing in the hilly interior of the island, we would travel by a horse-drawn wagon. Our tour included a stop at the luxurious Grand Hotel where we sipped a strawberry daiquiri and pretended to be rich.

The following day, Monday, September 7, Cindy and I once more set out on our bikes. We visited churches, graveyards, Fort Mackinac, and the Butterfly House, but they were only stops along the way to our ultimate destination and the beginning of a new and unique experience using automatic writing; we were ghost hunting.

After leaving the Butterfly House, we pedaled our bikes up the hill to Terrace Cottage. It was an unassuming-looking white house that had been a boardinghouse at the turn of the eighteenth century, now rented to college students who worked on the island during the summer break.

Cindy's friend told us that she had learned from a reliable source that a young lady who had committed suicide sometime in the early 1900s haunted the house. Several young men staying there for the past several summers refused to sleep in the turret-shaped room on the front of the house because they claimed to hear scratching on the window, while others reported a general feeling of a ghostly presence living there. That was all we knew, but that was all we needed to know to make the decision to pay a call on the ghost of Terrace Cottage. I had never seen a ghost, but my mind was open. Could we communicate with this ghost through automatic writing? We would soon find out.

We wanted to go inside and perhaps visit the room where the suicide had taken place, but there were people living there and we didn't think we would be welcomed if we told them that we were here to try to communicate with their resident ghost using something called automatic writing.

We settled for parking our bikes across the street and seating ourselves on the narrow curb facing the window of the turret-shaped room where a young girl once lived, died, and now perhaps haunts. Even the bright September sunshine could not dispel the eerie sadness that crept over us as we sat staring at the house and imagining what it must have been like to live there nearly one hundred years ago. However, there was also an intuitive feeling of excitement, a feeling that this could be the beginning of an adventure into another realm of existence.

I took out my pen and notebook and prayed for truth and protection. I whispered, "Nothing but good can come to me, nothing but good can come from me."

As I placed the pen to paper the pen instantly began to race across the page as Cindy looked on in shock. I put the pen down and swallowed hard. I couldn't believe what I was seeing. I had been doing automatic writing since 1972, and I had never experienced anything like this. We read the words together: **"Lady, we live forever. Fuck you. Enough of you feeble minded do-gooders."**

As far as I was concerned, this was it; I was ready to put my pen and pad away and head back to our bed and breakfast. This was *not* a beautiful, spiritual message like the ones I had been accustomed to receiving, and I would not tolerate that kind of language. I wouldn't tolerate it from the living, and I certainly was not about to tolerate it from an angry ghost.

"Let's go," I said to Cindy and started to put my notebook and pen in my fanny pack.

"No, Mom," she pleaded, "don't stop now. This could be interesting, give it another chance."

I reluctantly agreed and thought, "One more four-letter word and I'm out of here."

Again, I asked my guides for protection and warily put the pen to paper and let it roll. The feeling in my hand was so powerful that it sent chills throughout my body. The pen raced across the paper and wrote: **"Guides enter protection mode, giving the opportunity to grow."**

The words brought me comfort and seemed to validate Cindy's opinion that we should continue on and so we did. It wrote: **"Go away. Let me suffer in silence. God damn these people who try to save my soul. My soul is my business. If I chose Hell, so be it. Remember out of the fire and ashes of Hell arises the golden bird, the phoenix."**

I couldn't make sense of that statement, but continued to write, or I should say allowed the ghost, if that's what it was, to write. **"I'll give you this much lady, you don't frighten easily. We would like to frighten you, but your Guides protect you. Put this in writing Lady, suicide gets you nowhere. It solves nothing. If you die sad and angry, your spirit is trapped in sadness and anger. I am stuck here in this place and cannot escape. So go away, let me rot in Hell. If you think you write for me, its goose shit. Move on dummy and put that damn pen down. I told it not to write, but I can't make it stop."**

To be truthful, neither could I. My pen was zipping along with enormous power. **"The map of downtown is all wrong. The Golden Bird was there."** There was nothing on our map that indicated that anything called a Golden Bird was located in the town.

The spirit was right about one thing: I had no fear and was no longer shocked by the language. Cindy and I both felt nothing but sympathy for someone locked into such a miserable place.

Cindy said, "We are here to be your friend, we feel sorry for you."

I could feel the anger surging through my hand into the pen as it wrote: **"Don't say that you are my friends, I have no friends. Don't try to be friends with me. Love is overrated anyway. People should leave me and my house alone. Leave now and don't come back."**

Cindy said, "We want to stay for a while and talk to you. We want to get to know you better. We have enormous compassion for you. What is your name?"

"Dolly." The next few letters were difficult to read, but looked like **"Fumochmowery."** Later we wondered if the name could have been *Dotty* because t's look exactly the same as L's.

Cindy asked, "Where are you buried?"

And the writing replied: **"Dolly mocks you. Most people would be frightened. Carolyn and Cindy you belong in Hell."**

Cindy asked, "Why?" as we looked at each other and chuckled.

Dolly wrote: **"Because Dolly says so and I am NO Joke."**

We apologized as the writing continued: **"I'll give you this Lady, you believe in me and you are not afraid of me. That's better than most. Fuck you bitches, you make me furious. Go to Hell. Tell me how can your world hold to a belief system and a would-be God of Love? God is only an illusion of Love. My life was an illusion and the glory of Love is a joke. God teases us with lust and we call it love. I loved and my love betrayed me. God hates me. God loves only those who become slaves to Him. God is a slave driver in the first degree. My God, would we be copulating if God had not given us that strong desire? When we do, women are called a whore. They told me that God would send me to Hell. Could Hell torment me more than I was tormented by those who called me a harlot and a whore? Even if death takes me to Hell, it would be better than this. Mother is furious with me. I brought her shame, her friends shun her now and she is lonely. She blames me and she hates me.**

God hates me. My body is rotting in the ground and my soul is rotting in Hell."

Cindy and I were moved and saddened by the angry words forming on the paper. Cindy whispered, "We are so sorry for what you have been through. In this day and time it would probably be different. We feel enormous compassion for you and would like to know you better. We would like to know your whole story. Can you tell us more about your life? Would you tell us why you committed suicide? Would you be willing to tell us more about your lover, more about your mother, and most importantly, more about yourself?"

"Why should I tell you anything? You would end up calling me a whore like all the rest who claimed to be my friends. They were only my friends until they found out that I was in the family way and my lover was a married man. That makes me a whore and whores have no friends."

"Dolly," Cindy whispered, "we genuinely care and feel nothing but compassion for you and how you must feel. The emotions you have just expressed to us are the same feelings we would most likely have felt if we had been in your situation at that time in history. Attitudes have changed now and people are at least a little less judgmental than they were when your problems began. We would like to know more about your lover, how you met, what was his name, and why did he not stand by you and his unborn child when you needed him most."

Dolly wrote: **"His words were sweet poison. I don't know if I want to tell you, I don't know how to trust. I trusted too much and the wine was too strong. 'Sweet Dolly,' he said, 'you will someday be my wife, but you must wait.' 'But I carry your child inside me,' I cried. 'Soon I will show. Divorce your wife and marry me as you promised or I'll be called a fallen woman.' 'Oh my sweet Dolly,' he said, 'If you really love me you'll wait. My wife is also pregnant and if I divorce her now my career will be ruined. If you really loved me, you would not wish this for me. Wear this golden locket as a symbol of our love. Someday we'll be as free as this golden bird and we'll be together forever.'**

"His wife is coming, I have to hide in the pantry and climb out of the window. It's so cold tears freeze on my face. I believed him, I had been a fool and soon everyone would know. The humiliation is unbearable."

My pen seemed to slow a bit and then the powerful energy returned. As Dolly continued with her story: **"My mother is still furious with me. I brought shame upon her. Her friends shunned her and now she is lonely and blames me. She says she will never forgive me for that. She tells me the golden bird will never fly. Mother buys everything she likes, but she wouldn't buy music for my funeral. I wanted music, I love music. I tell you this; even poor people have music at their funeral. My mother is a bitch. Loving her so-called upstanding life more and being the wife of an upstanding man. John Wagner, my father's wealthy friend, did it to me the first time. I was only a child when he got me. God always favored him over me. God never calls a man a whore. He was bad, but God favored him, God blessed him with wealth while his ugly truth was hidden. I was the one who was sent away to this God-forsaken island. Now I'm supposed to forgive? I had rather burn in Hell forever than to forgive them."**

"Forgiveness, Dolly, is your only escape from your torment, withholding forgiveness doesn't hurt them, and it only chains you to your misery," I whispered. Once more the feeling in my hand changed somewhat. The writing was still strong, but the anger seemed to dissipate just a little.

The writing continued: **"Dolly is sure that the power of the pen is given to those who seek Truth but Truth is not always beautiful. Girls, you give me much to think about. If God is really Love and the path to peace is found in forgiveness, why do I not have the power over my anger? Why is love and forgiveness always just out of my reach? The truth is I fail at everything. Suppose I should try to tell you my story, wouldn't I fail at that also?"**

For a brief time the writing stopped and I wasn't sure it would begin again. I thought Dolly had left us. Then my pen felt completely different and wrote: **("God, if you are real, let me find you! If there is a God, take me in your arms and tell me that I am Not a whore, put on me the golden wings and allow the golden bird fly up from this hell."**

There followed another long pause in the writing and when it continued the feeling was different.

"God you are Real, you are with me. I hear the drums, I hear the music, and light pours upon my wretched soul. Say a prayer for me, let me help other girls learn from my

mistakes, let me tell them to give up men who only use them for their pleasure; to recognize when sweet words are poison and to know that Love has nothing to do with sex. When men tell you it is the same, believe them not. I am Not a whore, I only loved too much and blindly trusted that I was loved in return. Summer has ended, let the new season begin. But I want you to know that you will be a welcomed visitor to my house should you want to call on me again. Write my story. Tell the world that Dolly is Not a whore."

We agreed. We decided to gather as much information as possible from Dolly and find any public documents that might help to validate the story or fill in missing details. We whispered, "We love you, Dolly, and we know that you are *not* a whore!"

"You do not call me a whore like I thought you would. Maybe this writing is not so bad. You are on a level of peace. Your level does not call me a whore. The book is wrong, correct it. Put my words down on paper. I have feelings. You have summoned the Cosmos and the Cosmos tells me I must forgive and I will be forgiven. God upon Earth is God's gift of peace. God, I want peace, yet I cannot yet forgive completely, my love betrayed me, he called a whore. Pray for me. Pray that I might be able to forgive and be forgiven, find peace and fly away from this ugly place like the golden bird flying high and free. I think my mother still hates me. She says that the souls of sinners fall into the pit and there is never a way out. God lives in the Golden Kingdom and I cannot enter. You pray for me, you dare to be my friend. <u>You shall see my picture tomorrow, but you will not know me. The picture is not good.")</u>

There was a pause in the writing and then it began again.

"Listen, the music is different now. All things are different now. Girls laugh now at things once forbidden. The girls are girls I knew before. They will always come back. 'Girls, girls,' Papa would say, 'you should never laugh when men make ugly words.' Why does his anger not go away? Will it stay forever? Using this writing has released memories and emotions and my hate and anger explode. The power of the pen exhumes the mother of hate and shame. This is troublesome. I try to forgive and for a time it is better. I try to let my anger burn in Hell, but it leaps up and scorches me again and again. Why will it not leave me

forever? Why does God not put out the fire of anger forever?"

There was another pause and then: **"Dolly is sure that the power of the pen is given to those who seek Truth."**

People were giving us strange stares as they passed. It must have been a curious sight to see two ladies sitting on a curb writing in a tablet and talking to the air. And if they knew the truth? Well, I guess some things are best kept secret.

We said aloud, "Dolly, we have to leave you now, our presence is beginning to draw attention. Is it possible for you to write through us when we get back to the hotel?"

"I don't know. I don't know if I want to tell you any more."

We bid Dolly fond "farewell and God bless you," hopped on our bikes and headed back to the hotel. There was a lot of writing to decipher. This writing was reasonably clear, but like all of my automatic writing, all of the words run together, "L's" and "T's" look the same, "i's" and "e's" look the same and there is no punctuation. It would take quite a while to decipher.

As soon as we were back at the hotel, I took out my pen and paper and tried to put in the proper punctuation, cross the "t's" and dot the "i's." Cindy and I had discussed the questions we would like to ask Dolly. When I took out my pen and notebook again and started to write, the writing started out about something pertaining to our private lives and had nothing to do with Dolly. We were disappointed, thinking we had lost her. We asked, "Dolly, if you were here right now and were asked, 'what is your name and where do you live,' what would be your answer?"

The pen wrote: **"My name is Dolly and I live in Hell."**

Cindy and I looked at each other. I don't remember ever feeling such compassion for anyone in my life. This was truly a tormented soul. Cindy said, "Dolly, what can we do to help you?"

"Just pray for me that I am able to forgive and know the peace of a loving God. I do want to help other girls. I want you to write my story. I'll worry about Hell later."

Throughout the rest of my Labor Day trip to Michigan, and another in March 1999, Dolly relayed an intriguing story of early sexual molestation by a wealthy family friend, being sent away to Mackinac Island, love, pregnancy, and betrayal, of suffering and humiliation ultimately ending in her suicide in the turret room of Terrace Cottage. Her story would make a great novel, and I sometimes wonder if that's exactly what it was. The words came too fast for me to be making it up as I went along, so we assumed at the time it was true. The following year Cindy and I researched old newspapers and census reports, but found nothing for that time and that place. We were unable to locate any records for that period, that could prove or disprove Dolly's story, but we haven't given up hope.

However, there was a validation of sorts. The day after our first meeting with Dolly we visited the Island Book Store, located in the Main Street Center, where Cindy picked up a book on the history of Mackinac Island and decided to buy it. As she thumbed through the pages, she found a small photograph of Terrace Cottage, taken in 1901 or 1902, the time when Dolly would most likely have been living there. Although there were many people in the photo, we felt intuitively that one of them had to be Dolly. So just as she had mentioned in the writing, we had indeed seen her photograph and it wasn't "good" quality. Under a magnifying glass we examined the photo closely and found a young girl looking out of the window of the turret room, wearing a locket. Could the locket have been a golden bird, the Phoenix, given to her by her lover? We may never know for sure. We would love to research this story more fully sometime in the not-too-distant future.

In the meantime, we prayed for Dolly's soul, that she would be willing to forgive and move into the Light. I asked for Addy and Judi to pray for her also.

Then one day Dolly came through and thanked us for helping her accept that forgiveness was her ticket out of Hell. Her energy seemed uplifted and joyous, and she said that she had at last found a loving God. Her name still appears in my writing from time to time, always to express her appreciation and love. I hope someday her full story will be told. Her life reads like a novel.

Photo Credit: Mackinac State Historic Parks Collection

Chapter 20

My Mother, the Psychic

It never failed. Whenever I left town to be with one of my children, a crisis situation would develop with Mother, leaving my sister to handle it alone. Although this wasn't exactly a crisis, it was an interesting experience in the summer of 1998 when I took my granddaughter home to California after she had spent the summer with me. I had told Addy only that I would be taking Trisha home to California and that I would be away for about two weeks.

The day I left, Addy went to visit Mother, and while cleaning out her refrigerator, Mother told her that my father was talking to her. This was a bit strange as my father had been dead since May 1991. Addy said, "Oh really, what does he have to say?" Mother replied, "He said that we won't be seeing Carolyn for a while, she's somewhere in Arizona." Unbeknown to Addy, Trisha and I had a four-hour layover in Phoenix on the very day my father told my mother that I was somewhere in Arizona. Can Alzheimer's disease bring about psychic abilities?

Another strange thing happened while I was away. One day when Addy was with her, Mother started to sing "When it's Springtime in the Rockies, I'll be coming back *for* you, little sweetheart of the mountains with your bonnie eyes so blue." Mother remembered every word. She couldn't remember if she had eaten breakfast, but she knew every word to that song. I passed it off to a memory of hearing Kate Smith sing "Springtime in the Rockies" so many times long ago on her radio show, but Addy sensed there might be more.

I wondered if it was Alzheimer's disease or just the process of dying that seems to bring out latent psychic abilities. When my mother-in-law was in her last stages of Alzheimer's, she spoke frequently to her dead sister. Tim's aunt Gertrude also died of complications from Alzheimer's. She insisted that I set a place at the table for her deceased brother and sister and couldn't understand why I couldn't see them. My father did not have Alzheimer's, but when he was dying of Myasthenia Gravis, he spoke by name to each of his sisters, his brother who was killed in World War I, and to his mother. The only sister he didn't speak to was the one with whom he had been closest, the only one still living at the time.

This time while I was enjoying my Labor Day trip to Mackinac Island, Mother established contact with a more menacing spirit. Addy received an urgent call from the manager of Mother's assisted living complex. Her condition had changed radically. Mother had begun to hear voices and the sound of a baby crying prompted her to leave her apartment and roam around the parking lot looking into cars for the crying baby. Also, Mother told the resident nurse that someone had called and told her that my father had been in an auto accident and Mother went out to look for him. Alzheimer's is a cruel disease.

As soon as I arrived home from Michigan, Addy and I planned to meet at Mother's apartment and talk to the staff to see what we had to do next.

I arrived first and as soon as I entered the room and said, "Hello, Mother," she screamed at me, "Shut up, can't you see I'm on the telephone." She was holding an empty fist to her ear. I could see that she was upset so I shut up and sat down. The old familiar fire was back in her dark eyes and the sight took me back to an incident from my childhood. Mother was a soap opera junky. From the early days of radio, Stella Dallas, Helen Trent, and Ma Perkins were like members of the family, and there had to be complete silence when the radio was tuned to one of her programs.

On this particular day, which had to be a Monday because that was the day Mother washed clothes, I came home from school for lunch. Our kitchen on D Street was so narrow one had to pass through single file. But on washday when the old Maytag was pulled from the back porch into the kitchen and hooked to the sink, there was no room for anything else, so I ate lunch from the kitchen cabinet and listened to Ma Perkins. The Wheaties box was sitting on the kitchen cabinet along with a box of Duz laundry soap. The problem was both boxes were orange. Ma Perkins was in the middle of a trauma and weeping loudly. As Mother listened intently, she proceeded to dump Wheaties into the churning clothes. I called out, "Mother, you're ..." "Shut up!" she interrupted, "I want to hear my program!" The more I tried to tell her what she was doing, the madder she got. So I did as I was told, kept my mouth shut and giggled as Mother continued to pour the Wheaties into the washer, looking puzzled that there were no suds. When she finally discovered what she had done, she was furious with me for not stopping her. I had accepted a long time ago that I couldn't win with Mother, that I could either allow myself to get upset and suffer hurt feelings or I could laugh and accept that that was my mother. Most of the time I was able to laugh. What a mess that turned out to be. I pulled pasty Wheaties flakes from my pockets for weeks. In the years to come I would tell that story on Mother and she too would laugh.

Now I was being greeted by the same fiery little old Mother and it was kind of nice to see her now the way I remembered her best ... angry.

I tried again to speak to her, but she had that imaginary phone pressed to her ear and was having a conversation that sounded so real I was almost convinced there was really someone on the other end.

After a while I asked, "Who are you talking to?"

"I'm talking to Derwood, and it's long distance so shut up so I can hear what he's saying," she scolded.

"Derwood?" I thought for a moment and then remembered the story Mother had told me many times. Derwood was Mother's first boyfriend who used to ride his pony over to see her and her grandfather would always chase him away. I think Mother was only about twelve or thirteen at the time, and as far as I knew she had never seen him after they became adults.

The more I tried to have a conversation with Mother, the more upset with me she became so I decided to sit quietly and eavesdrop on Mother's conversation with Derwood as I waited for my sister to arrive.

When Addy finally arrived and spoke to Mother, she was also greeted with "Shut up, can't you see I'm on the telephone!" Addy and I exchanged glances, shrugged our shoulders, and started to discuss the situation when Mother's neighbor from across the hall came in. Mother's neighbor's husband had died of Alzheimer's several months before, and she always came over as soon as she saw Addy or me coming for a visit. She liked to keep us posted on Mother's condition as well as the latest complaints about the management of the facility.

The three of us began a conversation that annoyed Mother even more. "I can't hear anything," she barked, "with the three of you talking all the time." With that she went into the bathroom, just off the living room, and used the closed toilet for a chair, leaving the door open as she continued her conversation with Derwood.

Suddenly, she raised her imaginary phone, pointed it in my direction, and said in a demanding tone, "Carolyn, Derwood wants to talk to you."

"Oh, God," I said to Addy, "I don't know what to do." I tried everything to avoid it, but Mother was becoming more and more agitated. Finally, I gave in and decided that if it would calm her down a little I would speak to her dead boyfriend on her imaginary phone. Not only did she insist that I speak to him, but she insisted that I sit on the toilet seat to do it. It was hard to keep a straight face, especially when I could see Addy's shoulders shaking from trying to stifle her giggles and Mother's neighbor with her face buried in her hands. What a sight it was. I sat on the toilet seat holding an imaginary telephone talking to Mother's dead boyfriend while my sister and Mother's neighbor tried in vain to stifle their laughter and Mother sat with arms folded glaring at me.

Mother told us that Derwood told her not to take her medicine, that it was poison. I tried to tell her that Derwood told me to tell her to take her medicine. Mother became furious, called me a liar, and told me Derwood said for me to "go to Hell." When the nurse came in again with the medication, Mother was hostile with the nurse and refused medication. I had never met Derwood in person, but I certainly didn't like his spirit.

It was obvious that the time had come for Mother to leave her assisted living apartment and go into a nursing home that specialized in the treatment of Alzheimer's.

I found a nice facility close to me that had an Alzheimer's unit. However, in order to pay the additional cost of a nursing home, we had to sell Mother's house. In her better moments Mother would ask about her house many times during our conversation. She always held out hope that when she was better she would be able to return to her home. We knew we had to sell her house without telling her.

Fortunately the house sold quickly and a settlement date was set. I spent the night with Addy and we closed the deal the next day.

On my way home, I decided to stop by to see Mother. I found her crying and angry. She told me that someone had called her and told her that Addy and I had gone behind her back and sold her house. I couldn't imagine why one of her neighbors would do such a thing knowing her condition. I tried to put my arms around her to comfort her, but she pushed me away. I lied and told her that her house was just as she had left it and that when she was better we would take her back home. Mother would have none of it. She really knew that we had sold her home, but how did she find out? Had one of her neighbors actually called her or did she receive the information from another source?

I checked with the front desk as I was leaving to see if Mother had received any calls. The nurse told me that they had to have her phone disconnected because Mother had been placing 911 calls to the police telling them someone was in her house. That left only one explanation, Derwood.

Mother was transported by ambulance to the advanced Alzheimer's unit of a nursing home near me. I was glad that now I could take some of the pressure off of Addy. Now I would be the one who lived closer and would be on call whenever Mother presented a special problem.

Chapter 21

Mother Goes Home

Mother's arrival to the new facility was traumatic. Just before leaving her assisted living apartment she had become wild and belligerent with the nursing staff and was therefore sent to the unit of the nursing home that cared for patients with advanced Alzheimer's. It was like "Snake-Pit" revisited. Although all the patients were clean, well groomed, and given the best possible care, the sound of their screams and crying was almost more than I could handle, and Mother was even more upset. "You've put me in a crazy house," she cried. I didn't want to leave my mother in that place, but I had no choice.

However, with a new doctor prescribing a new medication and loving, attentive around-the-clock nursing care, Mother's condition seemed to improve. Although she still spoke to Derwood on her imaginary telephone and would go to the front door every night with purse in hand, refusing to go to her room, saying, "My husband is coming to take me home tonight," her disposition mellowed. It soon became obvious to me that she no longer belonged in what I had come to call the "screaming unit" of the nursing home. Granted, Mother had her problems, but compared to the patients in that unit, Mother was in good shape. I suggested and the staff agreed that Mother should be moved to the unit for less advanced stages of Alzheimer's.

Mother was in good physical condition with a strong heart and blood pressure like a teenager. Although I was glad she was not suffering physically, I prayed that something would take her before her Alzheimer's worsened to the degree that she would have to be transferred back to the "screaming unit" or worse yet became a screamer.

What a difference it made, not only for Mother but also for anyone who came to visit. Mother was popular with the entire staff. Not only were they fascinated by her telephone conversations, but also Mother used to draw pictures for them on her Etch-a-Sketch. Mother had artistic abilities all her life that remained with her even as Alzheimer's advanced.

I expected to be called often for emergencies, but there were surprisingly few. I visited Mother at all hours of the day or night and always found her well kept and reasonably happy. The only times she seemed upset was when Derwood was calling or when Daddy didn't come to take her home. Derwood reminded me of Flora's evil Richard. The only difference I could see was that Richard wrote and Derwood telephoned. But Richard and Derwood seemed to be coming from the same place and each had a single mission, to torment.

On February 26, 1999, Mother would celebrate her eighty-ninth birthday and we planned a little party. Our cousins from southwest Virginia wanted to come to visit Mother for her birthday, but the twenty-sixth was not convenient for them so we decided to have the party a few days earlier. That date was also more convenient for me. Cindy and I planned another short trip to Mackinac Island in early March to visit Dolly and see if she would be willing to provide us with more information about her life and also check in the local library for possible documentation that might prove or disprove Dolly's story.

On the day of the party the sun shone down on us, and God blessed us with a day more like April than February. God also gave us another gift; Derwood did not come to the party. Mother was in a happy mood and delighted to see Addy, Judi, our three cousins, and me. She couldn't remember names at first, but her face lit up the moment we walked through the door. We brought her a coconut cake, her favorite, and lots of gifts. She counted us "l, 2, 3, 4, 5, I've never had so many visitors," she beamed.

I had bought her a pants suit that she loved, but of course the slacks were much too long. When you are not quite five feet tall everything needs to be cut off. I measured the hem, pinned it up, and took the pants home to alter.

On February 26, her actual birthday, I brought the altered pants suit to her and found her agitated. Derwood was on the phone, and she wanted me to leave so she could hear what he had to say. She refused to try on the new pants and motioned for me to leave. Although I knew how unpredictable Alzheimer's disease could be, I was disappointed to find her hostile. I had planned to stay longer, but there was no point. I gave her a kiss on the forehead, said good-bye, and told her I was going to Michigan to visit Cindy and would see her as soon as I returned.

Mackinac Island

March 1999

The drive from Cindy's apartment in Clarkston to St. Igness was beautiful. Although Route 75 was clear and dry, snow-covered evergreens lined the highway. In the Upper Peninsula of Michigan, the snows of March and all the snow that accumulated during the months in between, covered the snow that had fallen in October.

Lake Heron was just beginning its spring thaw, which meant we could not cross the lake in a snowmobile or the ferry; we had to go by plane.

The plane looked like a kiddy ride at an amusement park and was about the size of my car, so when we squeezed in our luggage there was just enough room for the pilot, one passenger, and us. The flight was low and thrilling. Looking down I could see floating islands of ice tossing about in the choppy water, and the Round Island lighthouse stood out like a cardinal in a snowdrift. I saw the half-frozen harbor and the snow-covered island with its old mansions standing proud along the narrow streets. In the distance I spotted the steeple of the old church on the street where Dolly had lived and a shiver went through my body. We would soon be with our old friend, and I wondered if we would be welcome.

Fading light from the setting sun casts long shadows across the snow as we landed on the tiny airstrip. We were met by a horse-drawn wagon that reminded me of the song from Oklahoma, "That Shinny Little Surrey with the Fringe on Top."

The driver entertained us with song as the horse clip-clopped over the winding snow-covered trail. It was like a scene from *Dr. Zhivago.*

My painting in gouache of our ride from the airstrip to our B&B.

Our place of lodging had been carefully chosen. Cindy wanted to be within walking distance of Terrace Cottage so we could hike up for a visit or writing session with Dolly whenever we chose. Our cozy B&B was complete with a wood-burning fireplace, and from our bedroom window there was a view of Fort Mackinac.

Although it was almost dark we weren't ready to call it a day. We decided to take a walk up the street to Dolly's house to see if she was at home. I picked up my notebook and pen and we took off. Although the temperature was well below freezing and the snow crunched under our boots, we didn't feel the cold. By the time we reached St. Anne's Church and turned the corner, it was almost dark. As we climbed the hill to Terrace Cottage I could feel the elevator in my solar plexus and I knew that Dolly was near.

Cindy had recently learned from a friend that the ghost of Terrace Cottage took special delight in frightening young men who slept in her room, especially if she felt they had mistreated a young lady. A friend had told Cindy of one such incident that had occurred recently involving a young man who had just had a violent argument with his girlfriend. He went to bed that night in Dolly's room and soon came running down the stairway into the room where his friends were sleeping. He accused them of trying to frighten him with ghostly noises and the wispy appearance of an angry young girl dressed in a long gown. When it became obvious that his friends could not have done these things, he refused to ever again set foot in that room.

Now as the moon cast eerie shadows of leafless trees onto the turret-shaped room of Terrace Cottage we wondered if Dolly was watching us from her window. We wondered if we would be welcomed as promised or if perhaps Dolly had other plans for our visit.

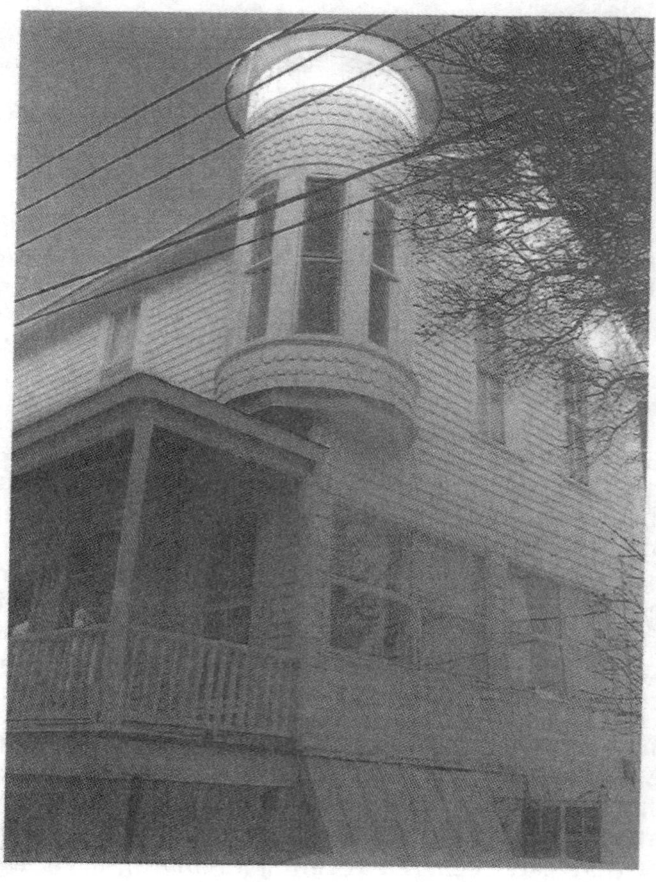

View of Dolly's room in March 1999

As I removed my gloves and tried to write, the pen froze to my fingers and the ink became solid in my pen. Only a few words appeared on the paper: **"Carolyn, put on your gloves and go home before your fingers fall off."** Of course, sitting on a frozen curb made another part of my anatomy rather numb. We decided that a nice cup of hot chocolate by the fireplace would be a wonderful way to end a perfect day.

The next morning from the comfort of our cozy bedroom we watched the sunrise paint a rainbow on the snow-covered hillside and a series of ancient streetlamps cast golden circles on the glistening snow, lighting the pathway leading to a lonely looking Fort Mackinac. Sights such as this bring out the artist in me, and in my mind I painted the picture.

After breakfast we walked along Main Street to the public library. Except for a few horse-drawn wagons, the streets were deserted, a far cry from the crowds of September. We stopped along the way to take some photos with my new digital camera, for every place I looked there was a picture begging to be painted.

The staff in the library was very helpful, but we could find nothing about the ghost of Terrace Cottage. The librarian told us that she had read about a suicide there at the turn of the twentieth century in the historic section of the local paper a number of years ago, but she couldn't remember exactly when. She suggested that we go to St. Igness where the newspaper office is located and go through their archives, or go to Lansing and look in the census report for the year 1900. A stop at St. Igness or Lansing was out of the question on this trip. We had already made arrangements to stay at our B&B until Monday morning. It's a long drive from St. Igness to Clarkston; Cindy had to return to work on Tuesday, and my plane was scheduled to leave Detroit Metro early Wednesday morning. We would have to postpone our trip to the newspaper office until another time.

As we left the library and took the long walk along the harbor toward Dolly's house I continued to take pictures. Mackinac Island in winter is a photographer's paradise.

Over the weekend Dolly provided many pages of automatic writing revealing new details of her life. If it was true, she had one heck of a life; if it was only a story, she certainly told a good one. However, there was some conflicting information, and she was vague when it came to names and dates.

Researching her story would be difficult and would have to be done on a future visit.

We waved good-bye to Dolly and Mackinac Island from the tiny plane, packed up Cindy's car in St. Igness, and headed south on Route 75 toward Clarkston.

We were almost home when Cindy's cell phone rang. It was her secretary calling using their 911 code. Cindy returned the call and was told that there was an emergency: "call your father immediately." Intuitively, we both knew that something had happened to Mother.

As soon as we reached Cindy's apartment, we called Tim. He told us that Mother had been rushed to Martha Jefferson Hospital by ambulance, that she had double pneumonia, and that she wasn't expected to live through the night.

I called the airlines to see if I could get out that evening, but nothing was available. From the window we could see snow coming down hard, accumulating fast, and the wind grew stronger by the minute. When we turned on the TV to see if we could get a weather report, we were informed that blizzard conditions were developing and snow was falling from Michigan to Virginia.

When I was finally able to reach Addy at the hospital, she confirmed that Mother's condition was grave and she was not expected to live through the night. We thought, "Here we go again, I leave town and Mother's condition brings an emergency for Addy to handle alone."

I spoke to Tim and Addy again on Tuesday morning and learned that Mother had surprised everyone by surviving the night, but they didn't think she could last more than a few more hours. Blizzard conditions forced Detroit Metro to cancel all flights. I was stuck here. Mother would die and I wouldn't be able to be with her to say good-bye. There was nothing I could do but pray. I placed the situation in God's hands and said, "Let thy will be done."

By Wednesday morning the roads had been cleared, and I was able to take the flight from Detroit that I had originally scheduled and flew home, not knowing what I would find.

Tim met me at Dulles. We drove home, dropped off my luggage, made a pit stop, and I was off to Martha Jefferson Hospital. Tim decided to wait at home.

When I entered the room, Mother looked more dead than alive, but she was still hanging on. Her eyes were glazed and she appeared to be paralyzed on her right side. Addy said that Mother had been in a coma since her arrival and when doctors had moved their hands close to her eyes she had not so much as blinked. Addy and her husband, Don, looked tired. They had been there since early Monday morning, and the strain of the ordeal was apparent.

I walked over to Mother's bed, took her hand, looked into her lifeless eyes, and said, "Mother, it's Carolyn, thank you for waiting for me." There was no sign of recognition. Then I said, "Mother, do you remember when you were in the nursing home and you used to wait at the door every night for Daddy to come to take you home? Well, he's on his way now to take you home, and you're going to be happier than you've been in a very long time." Addy and I looked at each other and knew that somewhere beyond the coma, beyond the Alzheimer's, Mother knew we were with her and knew what I had said, for a large tear came to her eye and trickled almost to her ear before we could wipe it away with a tissue. At that moment I felt for the first time that my mother loved me. She had never been keen on hugs or kisses or able to say "I love you," but she waited in pain on her deathbed for me to come before she let go and allowed Daddy to take her home. This was an expression of love much stronger than words or hugs.

Addy asked Don if he would like to take their car and go to my house and wait with Tim. He agreed and left.

As we sat there beside Mother, Addy filled me in on what had happened. After the nursing home called, she tried to call Tim but was unable to reach him until she was already in Charlottesville. Addy also told me of a strange incident that occurred in the emergency room. Addy said, "When I finally arrived at the hospital, I was told that a family member had been with Mother during the emergency room ordeal. They were very adamant about it so I assumed Tim had been notified by the nursing home and had been able to make it there. But when I reached him it was obvious that he knew nothing until my call."

Addy continued, "Later on, the chaplain said that a woman arrived with Mother in the emergency room and left when the chaplain arrived. There were no female family members anywhere near Charlottesville at the time." Addy was clearly puzzled.

"Oh, I'll bet I know who it was," I said. "It must have been Christine, or one of the nurses from Evergreene, they are all fond of Mother and whoever it was, was probably mistaken for a family member. I'll be sure to call and thank them for going with her in the ambulance and staying with her until the chaplain arrived."

As we sat there Addy asked me if I would do some automatic writing. I wrote at the top of the tablet, "March 10, 1999, Martha Jefferson Hospital, with Mother and Addy 3:40 P.M." It wrote: **"Father is here guiding your writing. All gather, so do not be afraid. She is not suffering the way you think. She is letting go of the body, but the body resists. Group gathered to take her home so we prepare her progress. Divine Spirit is giving her spirit power."**

We were comforted by the words and could feel that we were not alone in the room. There was a spiritual presence and we were at peace.

Then suddenly the lights went out and equipment stopped for a second; nurses and hospital personnel scurried about until the emergency generator kicked in and electric power was restored. We laughed and pondered the possibility that all the spiritual energy crammed into that little room had caused an electrical charge that short-circuited the entire hospital.

We looked up to see a solid black squirrel sitting on the windowsill peering into Mother's room. Mother would have liked that; she used to hand-feed her pet squirrels in her front yard.

We stayed with Mother until it was almost dark. We didn't know if Mother would surprise everyone and make it through another night, but Addy's fatigue was evident. She had been through a lot the last few days, and I thought it was time for her to come home with me and get a good night's sleep. Mother was in good hands; Daddy was with her. We kissed Mother on her forehead, said good-bye, and left the hospital.

Daddy must have come for Mother shortly after we left her room, for as soon as we walked through my door our husbands put out their arms and held us. The hospital had called and said that Mother had passed away. Mother would no longer have to wait at the nursing home door; Daddy had come and had taken her home.

Chapter 22

Springtime in the Rockies

As always, Addy and I tried to divide up responsibilities. Addy would take care of the funeral arrangements because she lived closer to the funeral home. The nursing home was closer to me so I would take care of closing out Mother's final expenses, gather her belongings, and say good-bye to the many nice people who had cared for her. I especially wanted to thank the woman who had accompanied Mother in the ambulance and remained with her in the emergency room until the chaplain arrived.

As I walked into the front door, I met Mother's favorite nurse, and she was crying. She sincerely cared for Mother and was saddened to learn that she had passed away. The hospital had already notified them, and she had Mother's belongings packed in a box. I was relieved that I didn't have to go to Mother's old room and gather them myself. I thanked her for doing that for me and also asked her if she had been the kind lady who had been with Mother in the ambulance and the emergency room. "No," she said, "it was a bad day around here, everybody was getting sick."

"Do you know who went with her?" I asked.

"I didn't see anybody go with her," she replied. "Check with the office, maybe they know."

When I went into the office to sign some papers and leave a check, I asked the administrator who had been with Mother in the ambulance; I would like to thank her. "No one from here," she said, looking puzzled. "It has been a rough week here, with viral pneumonia spreading throughout the place. Your mother was the first, but there were several others who followed. Your mother's roommate was admitted to the hospital shortly after your mother and she isn't expected to live. We would have loved to have been able to send someone with her, but there were too many emergencies here at the time."

"Could it have been someone from the rescue squad?" I asked.

She again looked puzzled and said, "I rather doubt it, we had to call them to come back for your mother's roommate, so they returned immediately after leaving your mother at the emergency room. Besides, I think they were both men and wearing the rescue squad uniform. I don't think they would be mistaken for a female relative."

This was strange. Who was the female claiming to be a family member? I guess that is something we'll never know.

Springtime in the Rockies

There was another mystifying event surrounding Mother's death. It was something that involved Addy more than me, so I asked her to write her account of the story. This is what she wrote:

The ravages of Alzheimer's had really begun to take away my mother's memory. Bit by bit, section by section, Mother's favorite memories were slipping away.

As I walked into her assisted care apartment, she was sitting in her old rocker that I had recently refurbished for her. Her eyes stared blankly out the window as she greeted me with that first puzzled look, and then after a moment she recognized me and called me by name and got it right on the first effort.

It was June of 1998. I asked her, "What are you doing?" to start our conversation. She asked me to hush because I was interfering with the beautiful music she was hearing. I strained my ears to try to hear what she was obviously hearing. There was no sound that I could determine. I told her I couldn't hear it, so she began humming the melody of the song. I asked her the words. She replied that she couldn't remember, and then her head turned slightly and she said, "They are singing it now." She slowly repeated the words to me as I sat there in awe of the new phenomena. It was so strange that she could remember every word of the song, and very little else.

"When it's springtime in the Rockies, I'll be coming back to you, little sweetheart of the mountains, with your bonny eyes so blue. Once again I'll say I love you, while the birds sing all the day, when it's springtime in the Rockies, in the Rockies far away."

Her eyes were distant and she was smiling. I somehow felt that this must have been a special song of hers and my late dad. I wondered then if she would leave us when it really was "springtime in the Rockies."

Time passed and Alzheimer's became much worse. In September Mother had to be transferred to a specialized Alzheimer's treatment center near my sister in Greene County, Virginia.

Mother had always been very healthy. The new treatments of massage therapy and special care seemed to help her thrive. Her arthritic knees were even better. My sister and I had no concerns over her physical health. Her mental state was quite different. She would talk to people we could not hear and hold regular conversations. She would become upset with us if we would not join her in talking to these people only she could hear.

In early March 1999, I received that call that no one wants to get. "Your mother is being transported to Martha Jefferson Hospital in Charlottesville, Virginia. Meet her in the emergency room." I was two hours away and my sister was stranded in a snowstorm in Michigan. My husband and I packed quickly to rush to Charlottesville.

When I got there, she had already been admitted to a special room. She was on 100% oxygen and breathing only with great difficulty. Her eyes stared blankly and there was no recognition in them as I leaned over her bed. She had been diagnosed with severe pneumonia and was yet to have another diagnosis of stroke to the left side of her brain.

Mother struggled with death as she waited for my sister to arrive. A tiny tear trickled down the side of her face, as we were both finally there together, trying to comfort her in some way. She waited until we left the room that evening for my sister's house, and then she passed away.

When we reached my sister's home, we were met with the words of her passing. I remember saying tearfully to my sister, "I guess it's springtime in the Rockies."

As funeral arrangements were made, I requested that special song on Mother's list of selections. At the last minute, the organist let me know that the song was not in her collection. I decided to let it go and prepare for the next day's funeral services. I did make a half-hearted attempt on the Internet to find the sheet music to no avail.

On the day of the funeral, I awakened with that song echoing in my mind. I passed the TV and CNN announced that, "It's springtime in the Rockies" and that part of the world was having a festival. I was shocked. I had no idea that it was really that time of the year for the Rockies. Our springtime comes on March 21. I decided to make one last effort to find the music. I had two hours to find sheet music for a 1927 song. I called my daughter because I had just learned recently that her mother-in-law also plays for services. She checked immediately, but was skeptical that she might have it in her collection. My daughter called back in five minutes. They had it.

The music was played at my mother's service. All of us who knew the story were moved and comforted by the gentle tones. I felt that Mother and Dad were indeed having their "springtime in the Rockies" and were together once again.

Chapter 23

The Book and Purple Mother

In August 2001 when I wrote the introduction to this book, I had no idea that it was a prophecy that would come to pass even before this book was completed. It was the encouragement or perhaps more aptly put the insistence of Addy, Judi, and Cindy that made me decide to put my experiences with automatic writing into written form.

They had become fascinated with my automatic writing, and every time we were together they would ask me to write. I would comply, somewhat reluctantly, and add, "You know you could do this yourself by following the procedures I followed when I first started." They would tell me they had tried without success and insisted that I had been given a special "gift" that I should use more often. On the occasions when Addy, Judi, and I were together and I would write, even my spirit guides would chastise me for not writing more often.

I knew I had become lazy about automatic writing and meditating. Of course I had plenty of excuses. First, Tim had retired, which changed my routine. I find it nearly impossible to meditate unless I'm alone in the house. Since automatic writing is only as good as the meditation that precedes it, my writing wasn't of good quality, often almost unreadable. Secondly, my youngest granddaughter, Trisha, has come to spend her summers with us since 1997, the summer she had just turned five, until the present time. Meditation and automatic writing are not things I feel comfortable doing with a child around. Thirdly, there was golf, which generally meant getting up early to meet friends at the tee box. All of these things were great fun, so I rarely gave automatic writing second thought.

Also during that time frame my vision was poor, and I felt uncomfortable driving seventy miles round-trip to Charlottesville unless I was certain that the weather conditions would be perfect. As a result, I stopped going to

Unity and taking classes and only rarely met with my Pineapple friends. My spiritual life was "out-of-sight, out-of-mind" unless Addy and Judi or Cindy and I were together. They would not allow me to give it up. Whenever I was with them, they would shove a notebook under my nose and say, "Write!"

Addy, Judi, and I decided to have a "ladyfest" and spend a few days at the beach place that once belonged to my parents and now belongs to Addy. Addy and her family had brought the old place back to life after years of neglect when my parents were too frail to maintain it properly. It was the perfect place to meditate and write without interruption.

We wanted to conduct an experiment to see if we could use automatic writing to help solve mysteries that had captured our interest. There was the case of a missing boy who had once lived near the beach place, the Jon Benet Ramsey case, and the latest, a young lady named Chandra Levy who was missing from her Washington, D.C., apartment. I wasn't sure if it would work, but I thought it would be interesting to try. Most of the time when I ask specific questions about specific people, my writing will take off on an entirely different subject so I wasn't expecting anything spectacular. At the top of the page I wrote: "July 8, 2001, 7:10 A.M. The beach place with Addy and Judi."

When we asked about the missing boy, the reply was that he was dead now, but had been alive for several years after his disappearance. When I asked, "Who abducted him?" There was no reply.

We asked about Jon Benet Ramsey and the reply was **"new information will surface in October."** In October the tabloids reported new clues; however, their legitimacy was debatable.

We asked about Chandra Levy. I asked where she might be found, and the response was not specific. However, the writing repeated, **"a clue, the blue box there is a blue box,"** some writing, which was unclear, then **"problem evidence found is (ex or eke) blue box."** There was some personal stuff about Mother, Daddy, and other family members and the two words, *"blue box,"* scattered throughout. This made no sense. However, two days after we returned home, police found a watch box being dumped in a trash can the day before Gary Condit's apartment was to be searched. When I first heard a report on the news that a watch box had been recovered, there was no mention of color. Addy called to tell me she had seen the box on television and sure enough *the box was blue.*

Although my writing did not give enough specific information that would lead to the perpetrators of the crimes, it was evident that the source of my writing knew about the criminal investigation. I don't know if there is a spiritual law that prevents my sources from revealing specific information or if they just choose not to but we concluded that my automatic writing probably could not be used to solve crimes. That doesn't mean that someone else's writing could not.

The blue box incident, combined with encouragement from Addy and Judi, brought me back to daily meditation and writing. I have found that when I prioritize my time, there is plenty of time for everything important to me. This is when I also decided to put my experiences into written form, not so much for publication, but to share my experiences with family and friends; trying to explain it verbally wasn't working. I would sometimes get sidetracked and leave out something vital or the whole conversation would take off in a different direction. So in August of 2001 I gathered up old notes and notebooks and began to write the story. Flora and I had thought of writing a book back in the seventies and fortunately I had retained the information. Looking back on the old days of automatic writing brought back many memories and lots of laughs.

Once I began to write my book I couldn't believe how rapidly it flowed. By the end of August, when Addy, Judi, and I met at Judi's for lunch I presented them with the first draft of the first three chapters.

Within only a few days something amazing happened: Addy began to write. She told me that by using the book to follow the procedure of meditation before writing had been the difference, and meditation became even more important to her than automatic writing.

Purple Mother

Her writing started out and has continued to be from an entity that calls herself "Purple Mother," and her words are always loving and inspirational. Neither of us had heard a term or name "Purple Mother," and we were puzzled. The one thing it proved to Addy was that the writing was not from her. Addy decided to go to the Internet to research the term "Purple Mother."

On Saturday, October 6, 2001, 3:34 p.m., I received an e-mail from Addy. Subject: "I found a Purple Mother."

The e-mail reads as follows: "There was a lady named Katherine Tingley (1847–1924), the 'Purple Mother,' a spirit medium with an interest in welfare work, who founded her center at Point Loma in California, a sort of American Adyar. I have no idea what this means, but the research is interesting. She worked closely with a woman by the name of Blavatsky, who founded some kind of basis for theosophical metaphysics and has done many writings I want to read. This article is part of something else which evidently has a long history in a religious and spiritual organization."

Was the spirit of Katherine Tingley writing through Addy? Could it be that Katherine Tingley was reincarnated as Addy?

In the months to come, Addy's research found that the two had much in common. Like Tingley, Addy has been drawn to volunteer her services to children's charities that include handicapped children and the American Red Cross. Also, Katherine Tingley had lived at one point in her life only a few miles from where Addy now lives, and there were other similarities in their personal lives. However, if Purple Mother is Katherine Tingley, she has changed her philosophy somewhat. She now expresses her feelings that crimes, especially against children, should not go unpunished and after September 11, she agreed with our government that those responsible should be brought to justice.

To me one of the wisest statements to come from the writing of Purple Mother was: **"Worry only in prayer, all other is unnecessary."**

❖❖❖

Shortly after Addy began to write, Judi soon followed suit. Judi's writing began much as mine began; she received embarrassing love letters from a gentleman from a former life and there were lots of giggles.

Building Crashes and 9/11

On September 11, 2001, I was out on the golf course when I received the news that shocked the world. Addy, who lives in Alexandria, saw the low-flying plane and knew intuitively it was heading for the Pentagon. Like everyone else we were shocked beyond belief and exchanged e-mails on a daily basis. On September 17, Addy sent me a short e-mail asking, "Remember this? On August 13 you sent me an e-mail containing a transcript of your writing and it said, **"George writing, building crashes, every body filled with water."** I had forgotten all about that message because at the time it came, it meant nothing. I grabbed my notebook and turned to the entry of August 13, and there it was as clear as could be. I also noticed that on August 15 the message was repeated. This time it was worded **"Divine Power gives courage, equips with purpose. We will guide and direct you, believe in us as we believe in you. Building collapse will elevate belief of others, bodies under water."**

In my e-mail reply I wrote, "Hit me over the head the next time I take a message lightly. When will I ever learn to trust what comes, even if it makes no sense, especially when it makes no sense. When I'm focused on receiving information on one subject and receive something entirely different, it should send up red flags."

After September 11, I understood the messages. However, I didn't understand the part about bodies being under water until it was revealed that there was a virtual lake of water at the bottom of the collapsed buildings due to burst pipes and water hoses. Bodies were indeed under water.

Chapter 24

Seven Young Men of the *Foam*

My daughter Cindy has a knack for coming up with interesting trips. Over the weekend of November 3, 2001, she invited me to go to Niagara on the Lake, Canada, to visit a haunted inn. Cindy's friend Adrienne would join us, and both girls reminded me more than once to bring my pen and notebook. It was rumored that a soldier from the War of 1812 haunted the Olde Angel Inn, and we hoped he would make himself known to us and perhaps communicate through my automatic writing. He did not disappoint us.

Although we were unable to find a room at the Olde Angel Inn, we were able to book a room in the cozy Moffat Inn only a few blocks away.

The girls were merciless. Every time I sat down, they shoved a notebook or scrap of paper under my nose and said, "Write!"

On the morning after our arrival, November 3, 2001, before there was an opportunity to meditate, Cindy handed me my notebook as Adrienne put a pen in my hand and said, "Write!"

As always, when I write without time for proper meditation, I said a little prayer for truth, wrote the date, "Nov. 3, 2001 8:05 A.M.," at the top of the paper, and my pen began to write. Much of it was scrawly and difficult to read, but here is some of what was written: **"Lessons will be truth level elevated. Ellen, Energy of seven boys call on you, Give us the gift of elevation. Seven young men will call upon you giving gift of spirit."**

It was a spectacular autumn day with temperatures reaching nearly sixty-five degrees. The golden trees lining the streets had not yet lost their foliage and sparkled in the brilliant Canadian sunshine as we window shopped in every store.

We decided to have an early lunch at the Angel Inn and see if we could make contact with its resident ghost as the girls kept a sharp eye for a group of seven young men. They even decided how the boys would be divided up. Adrienne and

Cindy said they would each take three and I could have the one left over. I told them if I could only have one, then I got first pick. They didn't agree.

Our encounter with the ghost of Captain Swayze provided raunchy humor, and we laughed until our sides were sore. We must have been quite a spectacle: an older lady sitting with her eyes half closed writing on the back of a brochure at a table in the crowded Angel Inn with two young women, doubled over with laughter as we read the mischievous messages the ghost had written.

November 3, 2001

Olde Angel Inn

Our delicious lunch and writing session lasted well into midafternoon, and it's a wonder we weren't asked to leave.

Finally, we decided to return to the stores where we had window shopped earlier to buy a few things we had admired. However, anytime we stopped for a little rest, the girls would once again shove a paper under my nose, put a pen in my hand, and say, "Write!" The girls also continued to make jokes about the seven guys they were going to meet.

At dusk Cindy drove me to Niagara Falls, and we witnessed the awesome beauty of nature enhanced by the ingenuity of man. The falls were beautiful in natural light, but were spectacular in the evening when colored spotlights turned them into a rainbow of cascading water.

As soon as we had dinner, the girls once more asked me to write. By this time I was tired and wrote only a few scrawly messages that seemed to be from frustrated guides of the tavern ghost, one called himself Dr. Gleason and the other Dudley. They were trying valiantly to reform a reluctant Captain Swayze and asked for our prayers. We obliged and fell sleep.

On the morning of November 4, the girls once more handed me my notebook and pen and said, "Write!" Again, without time to properly meditate, I said a short prayer and began. It was 9:26 a.m. When I wrote the question, "What do you have for us today?" Here is some of what was written: **"Lessons will be truth level elevated. Ellen, prepare yourself, Giving trust to us is important (drawing of cosmos flower) Energy will cry out to the belief system of others. Giving trust to us is important. Seven set sail, seven sailing, bad news. As you write you will learn of your Guides. Echoes will be heard from afar, lingering through the world, bringing energy. Crying echoes in the ether promising writing to the Girls. Everyone knows that Universal Law elevates those who seek loving truth. Truth is."**

There was more scrawling writing, and some writing that seemed to be from the horny ghost of Angel Inn and another reference to the seven boys. We laughed and joked about the seven boys all the way to breakfast.

After breakfast we decided to visit the old cemetery across the street from Moffat Inn. Adrienne had been doing a genealogy study and wanted to see if she could find family names among the tombstones in the cemetery behind St. Vincent DePaul's Catholic Church. Most of the tombstones were worn and the inscriptions difficult to read. We walked slowly, reading the faded inscriptions and names of those who had passed from this life so many years ago.

As we crossed a small path and entered the cemetery of St. Mark's Anglican Church, Cindy's pace suddenly quickened, leaving Adrienne and me in her wake. Adrienne and I laughed and commented that she looked like a girl on a mission. Cindy was drawn to a cemetery plot enclosed by a black iron fence containing a worn old tombstone, a relatively new marker, and seven small individual tombstones. We looked at each other in astonishment; there before us lay the graves of seven young men.

The marker reads:

On the evening of July 11, 1874 the sailing yacht Foam left Toronto headed for Niagara on the Lake. As darkness fell the wind freshened blowing heavily from the east. Guests from the Queen's Royal Hotel watched her lights flicker and disappear. Next morning like an arm reaching for heaven only the mast of the vessel showed above the breakers on the bar.

A typical centerboarder with light draught and low freeboard, Foam was an older yacht and laboured in the high seas running. Despite the heroic efforts of her crew all aboard were tragically lost.

Here rest seven young yachtsmen from the Royal Canadian Yacht Club, Toronto:

Charles E. Anderson, Robert C. Henderson, James H. Murray,
Charles V. W. Vernon, Vincent H. Taylor, Weir Anderson,
Phillipps Braddon.

We had found our *"seven boys."* Our jaws dropped as we realized this was a validation of the earlier writing. It was especially significant for Adrienne. Although Adrienne was open to automatic writing, this was her first experience of witnessing a validation, and this one came in one day. I believe this entire episode was a gift of truth to Adrienne. And even though Cindy and I had witnessed many validations in the past, when it happens, we still feel amazed at the wonder of it all and it leads us to the conclusion that there is much about the invisible world around us that we are only beginning to understand.

We stood in awe looking at the gravesite of the seven young men for a few minutes, offered a prayer, took a picture, and wrote down the names. Cindy and Adrienne spotted a bench where I could sit, handed me my notebook, and said, "Write!" I wrote at the top of the paper: "Nov. 4, 2001, 10:30 AM, in the cemetery. Found Seven Young Men who died at sea — ship the Foam." My pen wrote: **"You promise not to forget us. Love you girls, Giving us the opportunity to commune with those of the flesh. Come to us; believe in us, we are real. Carolyn, to us you are so young. To Cindy, we were younger than you when the mighty sea swallowed our bodies and released our souls. Adrienne, we love you. Souls of those who perish at sea abide with you. Your compassion for our plight Elevates our soul. Your compassion is a prayer for our souls and Elevates us into the Fullness of Spirit. Lovely ladies we love you. Come back to us and give of prayer. Every visit is a joy to those who have Legend."** Then, inexplicably the word **"Puppy"** appeared. I was puzzled by that unrelated word appearing at the bottom of the page until I looked up and saw a puppy racing toward me with a stick in his mouth. Immediate validation is rare and this was the second in one day.

We strolled over by the water's edge to look out over the now placid Niagara River that had swallowed up the yacht, *Foam*, and the bodies of the seven young men 127 years ago. Yet their souls live on and are eager to be remembered and eager to make contact with any of us who are willing to accept the reality of their existence.

But as always, daydreaming about the scene of July 1874 was not enough for the girls. Once more Cindy and Adrienne handed me my notebook and said, "Write!" So I sat down at a picnic table beside the lake and wrote at the top of the page: "11:20 A.M., Nov. 4, 2001, Seven Guys of the Foam, tell us about yourselves."

My pen wrote: **"Dear Girls, we love you. Elevating us. Sea bonds all who perish there. Come with us."** I wrote, "NOT NOW!"

This writing became a question-and-answer session. Cindy or Adrienne would ask a question and to my surprise the questions were, for the most part, answered.

Cindy said to the seven dead seamen, "Describe your experience, please."

My pen wrote: **"Lookout spotted the mighty wave charging down upon us, coming very fast, bullet speed. Power given us to write with you. You'll learn body is only a temporary vehicle. Educate yourselves in ways of the spirit."**

Question: "Do you miss your physical body?"

My pen wrote: **"Yes, that's why we yearn to come back. Those who do not miss the body need not return. Ellen, someday you'll understand why you chose to return, but it was not for body satisfaction. You returned to teach."**

The handwriting changed and became unclear. I don't think it was from the boys of the *Foam*; it was more likely the horny ghost of Angel Inn.

Question: "Anything else?"

My pen wrote: **"Dear Girls"** and drew a cosmos flower.

Question: "Are you still in the same state of limbo?"

My pen wrote: **"Levels within levels. Those of like nature abide on like level and will enter lower levels only to help. Jesus was sent to this level to help others elevate, but he was misunderstood."**

Question: "Are you out there also on levels?"

My pen wrote: **"Yes, but now we write questions for you. Why do you bring love to those you never knew? Why toll the bells ring?"**

The sound of church bells broke the silence. It was noon. I guess the spirits heard them also. **"Guides guide us through the narrow channel to safe harbor. Could you tell us why old Gods will no longer serve? Will you come back to visit again? Are you willing to take us with you when we leave?"**

We told them that we enjoyed visiting with them and we would love to come back to visit again, and if they would like to come back with us to see how the world has changed since 1874, we would be happy to have their company. As for why old Gods no longer serve, we told them we had no answer.

I began to think of why "old Gods no longer serve" and concluded that if science and religion were sincerely seeking truth, with no preconceived notions, I believe they would ultimately come to the same conclusions: their rivalry would become unnecessary and the Spirit of Truth would be found in both.

At 12:04 p.m. the pen wrote: **"Seven Boys of the Foam, Dear Adrienne, you hold the belief in the Love of the sea (cosmos flower) We will give you our story and give you energy."**

Adrienne asked, "Do you want your story published?"

My pen wrote: **"Yes, Yes, Yes. Give us the Gift of your talent; you'll see the beginning of a new life."**

We bid farewell to our seven boys of the *Foam* but reminded them that we would be delighted if they would join us for lunch at the Angel Inn.

Ghost in a Tree?

This photo was taken as we left the gravesite of the seven young men of the *Foam*. Could it be that the seven boys of the *Foam* accepted our invitation to join us?

Chapter 25

Return to Niagara on the Lake, Canada

As I said in my introduction to *Opening to Fullness of Spirit*, this book may have no end. It was after the first version was printed that Cindy and I made our second trip to Niagara on the Lake.

The "Boys of the *Foam*" reminded me on countless occasions through my writing that I had unfinished business in Niagara on the Lake. They wanted their story told, but frustratingly couldn't or chose not to furnish pertinent details of their life and death. I somehow expected the seven to dictate a word-by-word account of their personal lives, their tragic deaths, and perhaps give us a firsthand account of what their life was like in the spirit world. When this didn't happen, Cindy and I decided to return to Niagara on the Lake to see what we could glean from public records.

And so it was on Thursday, September 4, 2003, I drove to Erie, Pennsylvania, to meet Cindy. After spending a night at the picturesque Findlay Lake, we headed north, stopping briefly to tour Lily Dale, New York, then on to Niagara on the Lake and our boys of the *Foam*.

We had hoped to find a room once more at the cozy, hospitable Moffat Inn on Picton Street, where we were staying in November 2001, when the "boys of the *Foam*" first initiated contact with us. However, we had not made reservations, the streets were teeming with tourists and there was a "No Vacancy" sign on the door. Although we felt it would take a miracle to find a room at the Moffat, we decided to inquire anyway; after all, how could *we* not believe in miracles? To our delight there just happened to be one room available located in the basement. We took it. I was expecting a Laverne-and-Shirley-type room with walking feet our only view but that was not the case. It was a large inviting room complete with fireplace. Back once more in the Moffat Inn, we felt quite at home.

It was close to dinner time and Cindy couldn't wait to go to the Olde Angel Inn, dine on their delicious cuisine, soak in the happy atmosphere provided by both patrons and staff, but most of all find out if the shamelessly flirtatious Captain Swayze had anything interesting to tell us. Boy, did he ever!

The wry old captain had plenty to say, especially to Cindy. Even before our meal was served my pen raced across the paper with unusual strength and clarity.

At the top of the page I wrote: "Angel Inn, Sept. 5, 4:58 P.M." and the following message was received:

"Drove long way to see me, love you girl. Pardon my manners, but believing in me turns on my burners. Mother, please pardon me; we can't help it. The boys of the Foam came here with you trying to save my soul, but they ain't no angels either. Come with me to the land of the Guides to journey through time and see the sights and enjoy a brew or two with me. The Olde Angel is a great place to spend the hereafter. Never a dull moment. Doubts will fade when Truth appears. Ponder this m'lady, you and I could haunt this place together, opening the truth of life after death, where moments pass as years and years as moments. Be glad m'lady we had the good fortune to meet. Journey to the Light is long and hard and someday I'll bid adieu forever and leave the Olde Angel, but it will not come soon. Everyone's heaven is not the same. This place is the one for me. Come with me NOW. Just foolin' ya, the time is not yet written for ya. Bye the bye we'll meet again. The world now is wicked. Boys of the Foam love you too, but you're mine girl, ye are mine. Bless you; be back after we have our drink."

As we enjoyed a hearty meal of fish and chips and shepherd's pie, we read the old captain's words and tried to control our giggles. Immediately after our dishes were removed from the table I resumed my writing as I thought to myself "you've come a long way, baby." To think I was doing automatic writing in a restaurant crowded with laughing people when once automatic writing was my most carefully guarded secret. I smiled to myself as I wrote at the top of the page, "Sept. 5, 2003, 5:42 P.M." and received a message from a character identifying himself as Dudley. This was not the first time the name Dudley had appeared. In November 2001 while visiting the Angel Inn, Dudley had explained that he was a frustrated guide who was desperately trying to bring the unrepentant Captain Swayze to the Light.

My pen wrote: **"Dudley here, we have made some progress with Swayze, long way yet to go, but you have helped more than you know. Boys of the Foam came to visit, tried to level elevate Swayze, but he says he's an old bastard and fullness of spirit can come later. Ruler will give up."**

The phrase *"Ruler will give up"* appeared several times after that in my writing. I had no idea what it meant or of which ruler they were speaking. At that time, I wasn't sure what that phrase meant. That would come later. Was that what they meant? I'm not sure.

I assume the following is from Swayze, but he did not identify himself.

"Me thinks Level has elevated too much. Prospering world seeks to find me, but I am hard to catch. Book was kind to me, bless you. Power of the Spirit of the Girl makes me shake; I am trying to be a good boy. Must behave and that does not suit me."

The banter continued and concluded with **"Ruler will surrender."** Then: **"Dr. Gleason here, Boys of the Foam brought prayers for Swayze. Souls elevate through prayer. Lovely ladies, believe us, the group will elevate when none are left behind, but individuals must be responsible to themselves."**

The name "Dr. Gleason" also appeared in the writing in 2001, but we haven't a clue to his identity. Cindy and I finally theorized that he most likely is a guide who is with the boys of the *Foam*.

The writing continued: **"We are the Boys of the Foam and well bred. Carolyn Greer, come with us, we will be the writers to bring our own story to life. But never forget that we were once real living people with all the joys, sorrows and crowing that the best of you still experience. Ground buried our bodies, but freed our souls. Our journey to the Light is long and wearing, but you have brought light with you. Bless you. We regret the sorrow we caused by drink. The group has to pay the price, but you have given us the opportunity to speak. Brother perished and I'm to blame. We had too much rum and too much crowing. We are a collective group bringing with us collective guilt for our**

actions. Writing this could be our way to help others to know that dying drunk and crowing means there will be hell to pay. Group must do good deeds to elevate our level. Mothers wept in sorrow, fathers wept tears of anguish we brought to them. Mother's weeping spells are angering to Father. The crowd is wild in here, like the old days in Toronto. Girl has many admirers." Then, signed in large letters: **"Boys of the Foam."**

We said good-bye to the captain and his spirit companions, left the Olde Angel, and hurried to St. Mark's to pay a visit to our boys of the *Foam* before dark. As we passed the iron fence that guards their gravesite, we invited the boys to join us on the river's edge. We sat on a picnic bench close to the river overlooking the site of the tragedy and I wrote at the top of the page: "9/5/03 7:19 P.M." The writing began strong and clear:

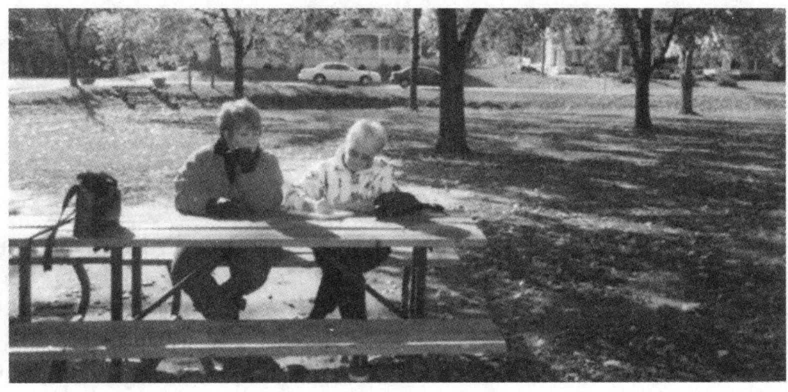

"Boys of the Foam welcome ye. Blessed be those who seek Truth. Joy is welling up within us that you have come back to us. Carolyn and Cindy, without you no one would be left to remember us. We visited Swayze and tried to help elevate his level, but he gave us the bird and mocked us. Book brought us together. Truth is not always beautiful. Group will try to write now. Give us energy with prayers. Joy with you provides us the Divine Connection. Girls, we open our eyes with you. The tide was in, the wind blew strong and the waves crashed over us but drowning was body only. Boys cry out, mast of our Foam turns, goes under and springs up again. No time to weep. We're in the

water and the night is black. We were very foolish; we thought we could weather this storm as we had so many others before. Our families were unaware of our voyage; it is only a small vessel...."

But as the last words appeared in my notebook, I could hear in the distance the faint sound of a trumpet playing taps. The haunting notes from Fort George drifted across the river to hover over the very spot where the *Foam* foundered and sank, sending the bodies of seven young men to their deaths and sending seven souls in search of peace. In my mind, it *was* July 11, 1874, and I *was* a guest of the Queen's Hotel, watching in horror the last flickering light from the *Foam* as it disappeared beneath the sea. Taps seemed a fitting tribute to the souls of our seven young men of the *Foam*.

In that moment of silence a fleeting picture of a half-forgotten memory flashed through my mind, a recurring dream from early childhood. In our lifetime, we have many thousand dreams, most of which are forgotten before breakfast, so why do I remember this one? Why do I remember it now? Could this somehow be the connecting link between the boys of the *Foam* and me? Could this explain why they chose *me* to contact and ask for help? Could it be we were connected in some way by the events that occurred on July 11, 1874?

As I closed my eyes it was easy to remember every detail. In the dream I am struggling in deep water and know there are others around me also struggling for life. Some distance in front of me, I can see the lights of a ship disappearing into the water. There is a feeling of helplessness; I am unable to save the others, unable to save myself. As a large wave of pale-green water envelopes me, I see a large fish swimming close to my face as I struggle to breathe. When my struggle ends, I find a blissful peace. Is this what it was like for the boys of the *Foam*?

With the last glimmer of daylight fading from the sky, Cindy spoke a few more words to our boys as we left the river. Walking in darkness through the cemetery on our way back to our cozy room in the Moffat Inn, I wondered how many unseen eyes of restless spirits were watching us, how many other souls might there be who, like the boys of the *Foam*, yearn to communicate, each with a story to tell.

Back in our room we tried to write more, but there was nothing legible. I guess the boys had already said good night.

In the morning when I tried again to write there was nothing legible for a time until finally the name **"Weir"** and **"Anderson years (or yearns), public book" and "we will tell you the answers to your questions, a revealing look at what it means to lose your body and begin a new life in another dimension. Guides alone can move between, bringing messages from one realm to another. It is not easy. We often want Guides but they are not always available."**

As we walked along Queen's Street to breakfast, the beauty of the flowers astounded us. From window boxes to the median that divided the street, to the little strip between the street and the sidewalk, every square inch of soil was ablaze with flowers.

After breakfast we drove to the NOL Library to try to uncover more details of the life and death of our seven young men of the *Foam*.

The library was staffed with ladies who were more than willing to go the extra mile to help us locate the information we desired and get us started using the microfilm machine. I watched Cindy's expressionless face as she slowly moved the film along. When at last her lips curled into a smile and her eyes widened, I knew she had found the burial record of our boys. Though difficult to decipher the old and faded writing, we were able to find a record of the burial of six of the seven young men.

Four bodies were buried on July 22, 1874; they are recorded as follows:

Robert C. Henderson, age 31, Barrister from Toronto

James H. Murray, age 23, (no vocation given) from Toronto

Charles C. W. Vernon, age 24 (or 34) no vocation given, from Toronto

Charles E. Anderson, age 18, (no vocation given) from Toronto

The following was written beneath the names:

The four preceding individuals were lost by the foundering of the yacht Foam on the night of July 11, 1874, off the mouth of the Niagara River, in a gale from the North East.

Several pages later we found the burial record of:

Vincent H. Taylor, 29 years (no trade listed) from Toronto, burial date August 3, 1874, and again it was written, "Drown off the yacht "Foam" off the mouth of the Niagara River in a gale from the North East, July 11, 1874."

Finally, there was the burial record of Phillipps Braddon, age 17 years, profession, R. C. Henderson's clerk, from Toronto, buried August 6, 1874, with another notation that he had drowned in the sinking of the *Foam* on July 11, 1874.

Three lines were left blank. We presumed they were reserved for the burial of Weir Anderson, but there was no entry. It appears Weir Anderson's body was never recovered.

6. Register of Burials, 1826 - 1979. (1 Vol.)

Burials.

Name.	Age.	Quality, Trade, or Profession.	Of what Place.	Date of Burial.	O[illegible]
[illegible]	2 Years	—	Buffalo	July 30th 1874	[illegible]
[illegible] Taylor	29 Years	—	Toronto	Aug 3rd 1874	[illegible]
[illegible] from off the Yatch "Foam" off the Mouth of the Niagara [illegible] from the North East, July 11th 1874. —					
[illegible]	17 Years	[illegible]	Toronto	Aug 6th 1874	[illegible]
[illegible] from off the Yatch "Foam" off the Mouth of the Niagara [illegible] from the North East, July 11th 1874. —					
[illegible] Clarke	6 Months	—	Niagara	Augt 18th 1874	[illegible]
[illegible] Clay	13 Years	—	St Catharines	Octr 12th 1874	[illegible]
[illegible]	36 Years	—	Niagara	Octr 24th 1874	[illegible]
[illegible]	81 Years	[illegible]	Queenston	Novr 1st 1874	[illegible]
[illegible] Stewart	63 Years	[illegible]	Niagara	Novr 3rd 1874	[illegible]

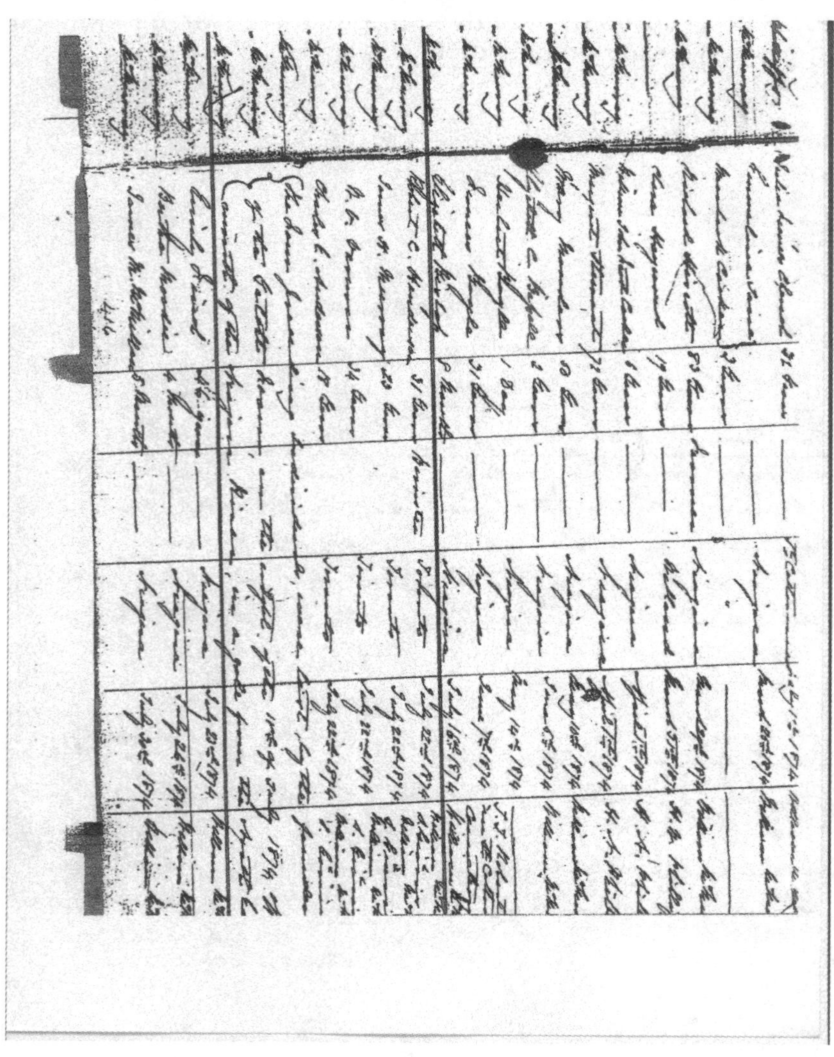

We returned to the Moffat Inn to a different room that was on ground level with sliding doors leading to a patio decorated with hanging baskets of impatience and overlooking a small alley path lined with black-eyed Susans. We decided to pick up a few snacks for lunch and do some writing outdoors in the warm sunshine.

I wrote at the top of the page, "Okay, here I am, it is 2:25 P.M. and I'm ready to hear whatever you have to say."

It wrote: **"Destiny brought us together to fulfill the great plan set forth over a hundred years ago. Opening to Fullness of Spirit found us. Guides answer our prayers. Writing his book is your mission. Murray writes now. Messengers bring us a picture, you are lovely ladies, reliable and intelligent. Divine Spirit watches over those on your level, allowing communication and peace. Boys of the Foam are bonded now, more like twins and twins and triplets, all arriving together in this new world of bodiless souls. Guides tell us you found our burial records. Bless you for your concern, Girls, you have freed us. Murray ... Murray pours his feeling freely, Robert holds his within. Weir was the clown. Weir here, it is good, you girls make me laugh. On the day we left Toronto little focus was given to weather, today it is easier ... Foam foundered in the water. I was hit in the back by the mast; body was broken. Bells rang out, but God's will was done, July was the time for us."**

The writing lost energy and became unreadable, so we decided to go back again to the Niagara River, sit once more at a picnic table, breathe in the fresh Canadian air, and see if our boys had anything more to say.

As we walked I began to realize how much the image in my mind of the Boys of the *Foam* was changing. When they first contacted us in November of 2001, I had pictured a group of well-mannered young gentlemen from well-to-do families who had set sail from the Toronto Yacht Club in a calm sea, in full daylight, unaware of the impending gale that would take them to their deaths. They were now, however, painting a very different picture. Now in my mind's eye I could see these usually intelligent, well-mannered young men indulging in too much rum, putting on a show of bravado, "crowing," fully aware of the approaching storm and with little left of daylight, recklessly setting forth on their ill-fated voyage from Toronto to Niagara on the Lake, a distance, as best I can calculate, of about thirty miles.

When we reached our picnic table, we witnessed a wedding taking place in the gazebo situated between our table and the water's edge, where a young couple, Christen and Daniel, exchanged wedding vows. I'm sure the couple was unaware of the uninvited guests both seen and unseen.

The boys reminded us again through the writing that they had consumed too much rum; they loved to drink, sail, find girls, and crow about their wealth and social status. They were on their way to meet Weir's girl by the Angel Inn. They admitted they were spoiled, were crowing, and the thought of setting sail with both darkness and a Nor'easter approaching might be less than a wise decision. However, they had no idea that that decision would soon leave them bodiless and yet still aware of everything that was going on around them. They watched helplessly as grief-stricken families and friends wept. Weir tried to console the girl he was supposed to meet, but his spirit voice fell on deaf ears. They told us there was a picture of them at the library, but we were unable to find it. Perhaps it is in a library in Toronto.

Then again the words **"Ruler will turn himself in"** appeared. I have no idea where that came from. It seemed unlikely to be something the boys would say. (However, only a few months later, Christmas day in fact, Sadam Hussein crawled out of a hole with his hands in the air.)

With that, the writing became unreadable, so Cindy and I decided to dine once more at the Old Angel and see what Captain Swayze had to say today. We enjoyed another delicious meal and were properly, or perhaps improperly, entertained by the outrageous, unrepentant ghost of Captain Swayze.

After dinner we returned to the Moffat for more writing. The writer of the following did not identify himself, but the writing was strong and clear. "8:00 p.m. Moffat Inn."

"Found the belief system of opening to fullness of spirit worthy of pursuit, focusing on love, joy and fullness of spiritual truth holds my interest better than boring sermons on guilt and fear. Boys of the Foam love you; pray that you will always welcome them. Ellen, long before we knew you, we knew of your Guides who have spoken of your mission. With joy we welcome you; your prayers are a welcome gift. Giving prayers tells us you are thinking of us. Ruler gives up. All the love, joy and fullness of spirit you send out come back to you. Focus on truth and the spirit of truth comes to you. Give truth to others and truth comes back to you. New body comes to those who seek the pleasures of the flesh; those who seek the pleasures of the soul opening to fullness of spirit can also come back in body form if they choose. Carolyn, Weir pours fullness of

spirit upon you. Actions belong to the past, learn from them and go forward a wiser soul. Level is elevating even now as we understand more. Joy level elevates physical energy. Love elevates peace energy. Fullness of Spirit elevates truth energy. Boys of the Foam bless you. Amen."

We had planned to get an early start on Saturday morning because I hoped to make the trip back to Virginia before dark. But as we wrote at 7:45 a.m. we received a message that changed our plans. The boys began to write individual messages.

"Robert Henderson gives fullness of spirit, money level will elevate, crowing, and crowing brings bad karma. Loved bluebirds. Charles Vernon, tell Girl all is well with the soul. We ask that you place flowers on our grave, we have never before had flowers on our grave."

Cindy and I were moved and surprised by their request. It was hard to believe that our boys had *never* before had flowers place on their graves. However, we were not about to leave Niagara without granting their request. Flowers were blooming everywhere, but we didn't want to take something that did not belong to us. The black-eyed Susans along the alley way seemed to be growing wild, so Cindy picked seven of them and we headed to the gravesite. Cindy placed a flower on the grave of each of the seven young men of the *Foam*, young men we were beginning to know so much better, young men with a story they yearned to tell.

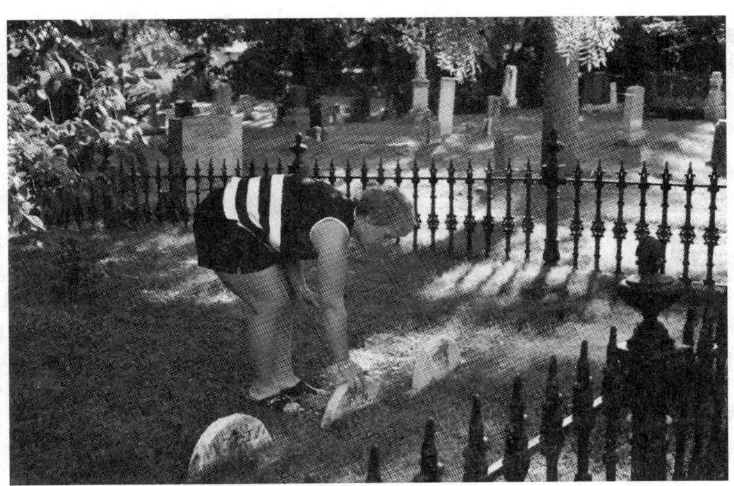

Charles E. Anderson, Robert C. Henderson, James H. Murray, Charles V. W. Vernon, Vincent H. Taylor, Phillipps Braddon, and Weir Anderson, whose body was lost forever beneath the waters of the Niagara River.

I found a bench, took out my tablet and pen, said a prayer, and began to write:

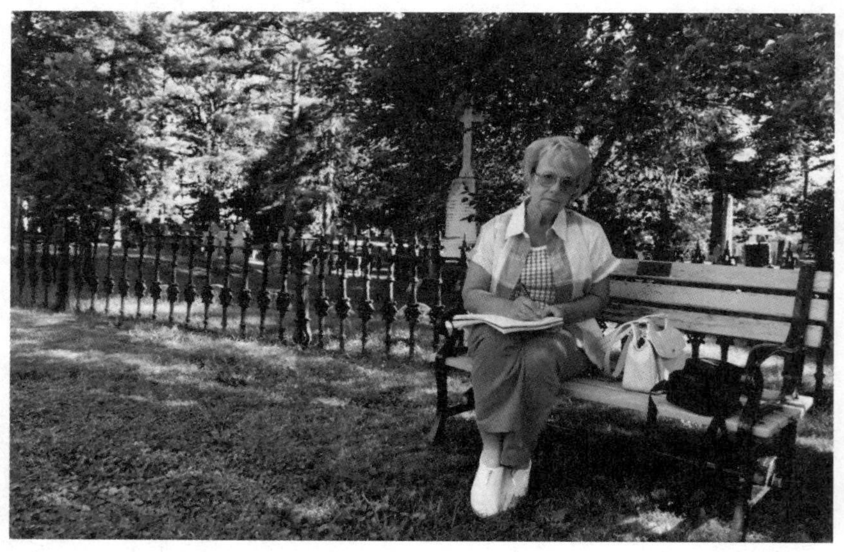

"Mary is working hard today." I looked up to see a lady inside St. Mark's cleaning up some wilted flowers and putting them in a trash bag. She looked at us curiously, as I continued to write:

"Your prayer for us and remembering us with flowers is appreciated more than you know. Boys of the Foam will live forever in your book. Promise to return again. Love flowers, they are a symbol of both the beauty and fragile nature of life. Boys of the Foam had yet to accomplish their missions in life. Unfulfilled missions create restless souls. Now that we are able to speak through you and warn others that drinking and crowing brings disaster, then our mission will be accomplished at least in part. Don't let your mission go undone. Robert Henderson here, power of

fullness of spirit is beyond measure. Rulers feel they have power, but the fullness of spirit is the real power. James Murray writes, please believe God's messengers of love, joy and fullness of spirit. Charles Anderson: pray for us until we meet again. We have wasted our bodies and can't find another to live again until we earn it. Weir Anderson: Drowning took my body, forever lost at sea, giving those who mourned my death nothing to bury. Phillipps Braddon: I was thrilled to be invited aboard the Foam. Charles Vernon: bless you. Fullness of Spirit provides much to those who seek truth. The spirit of Truth is the best teacher. Pruning prepares us for new life. Cindy has been pruned; new life will follow. Vincent Taylor: We love you. Truth level provides guides. Boldness is not necessary to prove manhood. Our boldness killed us before our mission was completed and left us bound to this lonely bed for what we thought would be eternity. Bless you for giving us another chance to speak. Bless you; we hope you will come back again."

I asked, "Anything else before we leave?"

"We prove to the world death of the body is not death of the soul. Until we meet again we bid you well. You are truly our friends."

Cindy and I returned to our homes feeling we had learned much from our trip, but it also left us with many unanswered questions. In November of 2001, when we made our first visit to Niagara on the Lake, we had never heard of seven young men who had perished in the sinking of a yacht called the *Foam* in 1874. They came to us, they initiated the contact, first at the Moffat Inn in my writing, and later they seemed to lead us to their gravesite. What might we learn from that? For me it validated the idea that there is a whole other world out there of invisible, intelligent energy, able to communicate from time to time with those who are willing to open their minds. The experience with Dolly on Mackinac Island was somewhat different. We initiated the contact; we went to her house seeking communication. However, there was one thing they had in common; they both had messages of warning to the living. Dolly warned that suicide did not accomplish the oblivion she sought; rather she was even more miserable after her suicide. The boys' message was a warning not to "drink and crow," that dying in a drunken state left their souls in a state of unrest. As for the unrepentant Captain Swayze, he seems to be perfectly happy to spend eternity entertaining guests of the Olde Angel Inn.

And even more questions: Are these souls speaking from purgatory? Is purgatory a place of punishment or a place of learning? So many times when I have asked about newly departed loved ones, my guides have answered that they are "in school" or that a particular person is on the "life review" level. Does purgatory, like schools, have levels? How many other restless souls are out there longing to be heard and what might we learn from them? How many others are there who are willing to listen? Could you be one of them?

Chapter 26

Conclusions: April 2002

Just when I thought the final chapter of this book had been written, something happened that forced me to rethink my conclusions regarding automatic writing. Cindy began to write and it wasn't good.

Over the years Cindy had tried many times to do automatic writing and received nothing. In early January 2002, after returning from church, Cindy had the feeling she would be able to do automatic writing, and she was right; it came quickly and clearly. Her automatic writing, though different from her own handwriting, was clear, the spelling was correct, and I felt certain her writing would yield great insights into Truth. Not only could Cindy, Addy, Judi, and I exchange messages just as I had exchanged messages with Flora and Mildred in the early days, but her experience provided the perfect ending to my book. "Cindy learns to write and we all live happily ever after." Wrong!

Cindy's automatic writing began with stories of past-life experiences that read like an epic novel, but progressed to predictions of a coming romance at a specific time in a specific place. This proved to be untrue and Cindy challenged the writer to prove himself. Instead of receiving a validation she received profane insults. The entity identified himself as Paul, and it was like Flora's evil Richard revisited.

I advised Cindy to come home for a short visit and we would perform an exorcism. I had complete confidence that when surrounded by strong, powerful love energy, the evil Paul would be exorcised just as easily as Flora and I were able to exorcise the evil Richard.

I asked my Pineapple friend, Nancy, to come to my house to help Cindy and also invited Addy and Judi to visit so that all of us could contribute positive energy to exorcise Paul from Cindy's writing. Nancy suggested using holy water, so we made our own using Nancy's recipe. Nancy's recipe is pouring water into a pan, turning the burner on high and boiling the hell out of it, and then saying a prayer over it. (Go ahead and laugh, we did.) Nancy also suggested that we borrow another Catholic custom using the sign of the cross along with the holy water.

We gathered in my small room where I have my computer and meditation chair and where I do much of my automatic writing. We meditated and prayed that Paul would find peace in the light of God, and for a time we thought we had succeeded. But Paul returned in a few days to deliver messages that were even more threatening and uglier than they had been previously. At that point, Cindy decided to give up writing.

I never thought that I had any special "gift" and felt that automatic writing was a natural process open to all. After Cindy's experience I began to believe that automatic writing is not for everyone. Why would Paul choose Cindy and Richard choose Flora? It is not that like attracts like; Flora and Cindy are both kind and loving people. If I knew why they received vulgar insults while Addy receives loving messages from Purple Mother, I would tell you what to do to avoid that experience. As I don't know the answer to the problem I would only suggest that if you should try automatic writing and receive even one vulgar or insulting word, put down your pen immediately. Just as you would not tolerate that kind of behavior from those around you in the physical body you should not put up with it from those around you in the spirit world.

I don't know if Cindy will try automatic writing again in the future, but I know she is not afraid of it. I have asked her to write a little postscript to this book explaining her own experiences and her own feelings on the subject and I have asked the same of Flora, Mildred, Addy, Judi, and Nancy. It seems everyone's experience is uniquely their own and if you should attempt automatic writing someday, try to avoid all expectations of what your experience will be. Addy has received from only one messenger, the wise and loving Purple Mother; Nancy receives from two entities, Con and Ideam; while I have received from a multitude starting with John. Although Cosmos has been with me most often, others have identified themselves from the life of Ellen, her husband, John, and her son Edward; George Darby Moss, the poet; Rolling Guide, the Native American; Sullivan Seagull; and most recently Boys of the *Foam*. This morning's message was:

"Divine Spirit Gives you Level Elevation Given only to those who have persevered in the name of Truth. Our final chapter is written today."

My own experience has taught me many lessons, and if I had it to do over again I wouldn't change a thing. In my opinion learning to do automatic writing is like learning to use a computer to tap into the Internet. There is a universe of knowledge out there, some of it wonderful and enlightening, but just as on the Internet there are predators seeking perverted satisfaction from terrorizing innocent people, there are predators in the spirit world. Would I throw away my computer if I found an unsolicited ugly message or a virus in my e-mail? No, I would simply delete it and try to install a better filtering system to protect myself in the future. I believe the filtering system of the spirit world is prayer and meditation.

The following verse from John 16:13 puts into a nutshell my entire experience with automatic writing: *"When the Spirit of Truth comes, he will guide you into all the truth; for he will not speak on his own, but will speak whatever he hears, and he will declare to you the things that are to come."*

When I read this scripture back in 1972, I overlooked this promise God gave us. In the early days of automatic writing when events would occur that had been written in my notebook, I would question its value. Why write about a coming event, especially one that brings suffering, if there is nothing I can do to prevent it? I now realize that preventing the event was not the purpose of the writing. The purpose of the prophecies was to validate that the words were not *from* me but *through* me, not a part of *my* subconscious mind but a gift from the Spirit of Truth who is sent to all who seek Fullness of Spirit. The purpose of the poetry was not to bring the world beautiful poetry from *me*, but to open my mind to the unlimited possibilities that come to those who seek. I believe I started to put everything in motion on Easter Sunday of 1971 when I arched my neck, shook my fist at God, and cried out for Truth. God answered my prayer, He sent the Spirit of Truth. I also believe that the Spirit of Truth will not be denied anyone who is an open-minded seeker.

My writing has also told me over the years, **"Translations and interpretations of Holy Books have been taught by rote. Religion taught by rote is not religion; it is a doctrine or dogma written by men inspired by political gain.**

Experiencing God's presence in a personal way teaches us best, for merely <u>believing in</u> God does not compare to <u>knowing</u> God."

It seems to me now that wars are perpetuated by doctrine taught by rote and followed in blind faith. Now their young strap explosives to their bodies in order to murder others. The doctrine taught by rote also seems to have been the basis of the Inquisition and Christian Crusaders of old who marched into foreign lands, fought, and killed not really for genuine religious conviction but for a doctrine taught by rote.

Today is Good Friday, 2002. Yesterday suicide bombers exploded themselves in the middle of a crowded room where people of the Jewish faith celebrated Sadder. Today Israeli tanks thunder into Palestinian territory, and war rages once more in the Holy Land, all in the name of religious doctrines taught by rote.

Dead Sea Scrolls

Long ago I wondered when man first began to receive and write messages from the spirit world. There are hints throughout the Bible. From the Old Testament, Moses receives the Ten Commandments and there was the case of the mysterious "handwriting on the wall." In the New Testament, Jesus takes his finger and writes in the sand. As we all know the Bible was not written at the time of Jesus, and the Dead Sea Scrolls were only uncovered in 1947. Who wrote the Bible and when did they write it? I recently watched a documentary "Who Wrote the Bible?" on the Discovery Channel and one thing struck me more than anything else. The Dead Sea Scrolls were written as if it was one long word. Like my automatic writing, there is no break between words, no punctuation, no breaks between sentences or paragraphs. Could it be the Dead Sea Scrolls were dictated from Spirit and was an ancient form of automatic writing? We may never know for sure, but it's an interesting thought. Also, much power is given to the interpreter and the one who decides which is God's word to be included in the Bible and who decides what should be left out. In the year AD 313 the Emperor Constantine, who was not even a biblical student, called for the Council of Nicea to decide what scripture would be canonized and which should be left out. The Nicene Creed and the Apostles' Creed were affirmed as "orthodox" and Gnostic scripture declared heretical. The Emperor Constantine may have thought himself God, but few people accept that premise.

Sunday will be the third day after Good Friday, and the Christian world will once again celebrate the resurrection of Jesus. On Easter Sunday of 1971, I thought I doubted my faith, now I know I only doubted the doctrine taught by rote. Today I know Jesus's message of Love is real and lives forever.

In my attic are boxes of notebooks that would fill thousands of pages but this book is not about my writing and me; this book is about you and the writing that you have yet to enter into your journal of life.

Should you decide to try automatic writing, there are some things you should keep in mind:

1. Take it seriously. It is not a fortune-telling game or to be used to spy on others.
2. Always begin with prayer and meditation. If you have never meditated there are many good tapes and books available. I would suggest you spend about fifteen or twenty minutes a day in prayer and meditation for a week or so before you first place pen to paper.
3. Write at the top of the page the date, time, and place of your writing and always ask if your guides come in the name of the Spirit of Truth.
4. Beware of the evil ones of the spirit world. Although they are a part of the Truth we must learn, do not allow them to use you as their instrument.
5. If something that seems strange or without meaning should appear on your paper continue to write. Remember, it could be a validation of your writing. Most of the things that made no sense at the time they appeared turned out to be some of the most significant validations of Truth. Don't be afraid to ask for validation.

THIS BOOK IS DEDICATED TO THE SPIRIT OF TRUTH WHO BRINGS FULLNESS OF SPIRIT TO ALL WHO SEEK

June 2004, Addendum to My Conclusions

Through the years I have received many validations of messages received in my writing, when prophecies come to pass, such as blazing fires in Louisiana appearing in the headlines of the *Washington Star & Daily News*; a seagull appearing on a child's windowsill, and finding the gravesite of seven young men who perished in the sinking of their yacht in 1874, I am still amazed. However, these pale in comparison to the validation that I am receiving now as I read a book by master hypnotherapist Michael Newton, Ph.D. In his book *Journey of the Soul, Case Studies of Life Between Lives*, he mentions "levels" and "elevating ones level," of "schools" of higher learning in the spirit world of souls. This book was first published in 1994 and uses the same terminology as my Spirit Guides used in 1972 and still use today. Also, I sought the "white" light and was disappointed that I only found a *purple* light. In his book, Dr. Newton's subjects have stated that colored lights are "Classification Models for Soul Development Levels." White is Level 1, the Beginner; Level II is off-white (reddish shades, ultimately turning into traces of yellow). Level III, Intermediate, is solid yellow (a deep gold with no traces of white). Level IV is Upper Intermediate, a Junior Guide, dark yellow (a deep gold, ultimately turning into traces of blue). Level V: Advanced, a Senior Guide (light blue, with no traces of yellow, ultimately turning into traces of purple). Level VI: Highly Advanced Master Guide (dark bluish-*purple*, surrounded by radiant light). It seems my "deep *purple*" meditation light was from a Master Guide.

When I read this I questioned why an ordinary person such as I would receive guidance from a Master Guide. I think the answer comes with the intensity of my desire, expressed in my 1971 Easter experience.

Dr. Newton states in his book that "Aside from the developmental level, I look at the intensity of individual desire as another consideration in the frequency of appearance and form of assistance one receives from his or her guide during life." My desire in 1971 was, and remains to this day, intense.

The title of my book, *Opening to Fullness of Spirit*, came from instructions given me during my masterminding prayer group. I was instructed that "fullness of spirit" was the *only* thing I need ask for in prayer. At that time and even now I have pondered the exact meaning of *fullness of spirit*. In Dr. Newton's book he states: "Different avenues of approach to learning eventually bring all of us to the same end in acquiring *spiritual wholeness*." To me this is the perfect definition of *fullness of spirit* and the quest for this level is the purpose of life, whether we know it or not and is the underlying reason my book was written.

If I were to summarize into three statements the most important messages I have received during my lifetime of automatic writing it would be these: (1) My purpose for being is to "elevate my spiritual level"; (2) Allow no individual, no dogma, no organization to impede my personal pursuit of spiritual fulfillment. Recognize the roadblocks for what they are, bless them, but pass them by; and (3) When praying for myself and others, pray only for Fullness of Spirit, God will take care of the particulars.

I would also like to add that over the years there have been about two hundred people who have read my book. I have asked them to share some of their personal experiences with me, and I have a bulging file with awesome stories that could itself become a book. Out of the numerous letters there were only two that called me names such as heretic, blasphemous, a witch, and a few other unmentionable words. Skeptics always sound intellectually superior even though for the most part they are people who have closed their minds to anything that conflicts with the things they have been taught all their lives. Although closed minds are a sad thing, I understand where they are coming from; before 1972 I might have felt the same way.

And so to you who have taken the time to read of my experiences I would like to say thank you for opening your mind and allowing me to share my spiritual adventure with you. I would love to hear from anyone who would feel comfortable sharing with me personal stories of spiritual encounters. My home address and e-mail address are on the back cover and I would love to hear from you.

I send all of you Love, Joy, and Fullness of Spirit.

Epilogue

Flora

April 2002

What a wonderful nostalgic few hours I've had reliving the early days of automatic writing. Carolyn's manuscript brought to life again the experiences that she and I shared during the early 1970s.

I'll always remember the fun we had deciphering the automatic writing that Carolyn received. She had no idea what she was writing because the letters came fast and furious and they all ran together with no punctuation, no capitals, and no paragraphs. Many times it was sprawled all over the page reaching above and below the lines.

While my automatic writing ceased, Carolyn's continued to inform and to predict news stories, disasters, and revelations. Once again we were on the telephone in awe of their writings; for example, the Oval Room; the blazing fires in Louisiana; the warning of the bombs in the flowers at the second inauguration of President Nixon. (This information was passed on to a member of the Capitol police who took it seriously. We will never know if anything was discovered.) All of these plus the revelation about Sullivan Seagull. If I hadn't been witness to all of these events, I might have doubted that it really happened.

Of all of Carolyn's messages, my favorites are the poems, "Truth," "Lies," and "Memory." I love to read them over and over again. One other spiritual message I always liked revealed in part, "I am as vapor and you are as water. Someday I'll be as water and you will be as vapor." A validation of reincarnation?

Over the years I have tried to write automatically just for the fun of it, but I still have the same old problem. I never take time to meditate beforehand, and I try to fit the writing in between other things I want to do. Still no patience for it.

I tell myself patience, Flora, patience, try again. Then the procrastinator in me promises, "all right, all right, I'll try tomorrow ... maybe."

While looking through my old automatic writing papers, I found a letter from Robert Inverness, supposedly my husband during the 1800s.

I wrote: "Am I going to have a new spirit write to me?"

Answer: "Yes, another spirit named Robert Inverness. Robert loves you. Robert was your husband and he loved you very much. Robert died in a duel with Richard Battleman. Flora died by accident in the Battleman *duel. Robert loved Flora and Flora loved Richard. Robert errr in the year 1882 in Inverness, Scotland."*

So that's what happened to Flora and Richard? Perhaps someday I'll take up my pen and discover more characters in a past life, but for now, I'll live in the present and enjoy all that it offers.

Mildred

April 29, 2002

I am now eighty-four years old and have forgotten many things, but I'll always remember well a telephone call to my workplace in April 1972 from Carolyn saying, "Come by as soon as you can, I must tell you something." We had shared so much. We taught Sunday School to junior high kids and after class, five or six of us teachers would discuss many things, the Bible, the kids, current events, etc. In the total Sunday School, we had six hundred children. We had great teachers. Some worked for NASA that was in our area, another for National Geographic, and one with ocean research. It was a wonderful time, young lives, good families.

When I arrived at Carolyn's she was very excited. She said she had been reading Ruth Montgomery's book and decided to try automatic writing and had received a message. It was the beginning of a long and most interesting journey for her and I am so happy she is sharing it in this book.

She urged me to try also and I did some. Usually it was a message from my husband's mother saying, "God loves you." And of course, there was the experience with my sister-in-law Hattie.

Carolyn was willing to spend more time in research and practice than I. Flora was also receiving messages and helped Carolyn in researching facts given to her. They found messages of reincarnation and explored names of people mentioned in her writings. Some were found and others were not.

The day we visited the minister to find his opinion, I decided not to pursue automatic writing further, not that I doubted this gift but I had a busy, busy life and did not wish to devote the time and energy needed.

The Dalys moved to Virginia and amazingly Flora followed later. We still stay in touch and I loved hearing of Carolyn's writing and the progress she was making in her pursuit of truth.

I moved to Florida in 1979 but visited Carolyn when we returned to visit in the Virginia area. She and Tim visited us once in Florida. We have corresponded over about twenty-five years. Have I ever doubted that Carolyn has this gift? NEVER! Do I know from my own experience and what I have witnessed that every word she has written in this book is true? Absolutely!

It is a fascinating book that makes one wonder, how close are the spirits to us? Why do we doubt facts like the ones presented here?

It has been a long interesting experience for Carolyn, and I am glad to have been a part of it.

Addy

When my sister, Carolyn, told me of her automatic writing skills back in the seventies, I never doubted it for a moment. After I saw some of her notes, I was sure she was on to something special. We were not close while growing up due to my propensity to be the bratty little sister. I was surprised that independently, later on in life, we had both come to very similar beliefs and had secretly tucked those new beliefs away for fear of ridicule. We both had been carefully raised with the fire-and-brimstone teachings of the Southern Baptist faith.

I immediately tried automatic writing myself without success. All I kept getting was the word "mother" over and over again. I threw my pen down in disgust. After reading the first few chapters of Carolyn's book, which she began in August of 2001, I decided that I had not been attempting the writing in a proper frame of mind. I tried again.

Now the first few scribbles (and they definitely were scribbles) began to read "purple mother," which again I found quite strange. Another phrase said, "play the tape." I took the hint and began to seriously meditate with music just prior to attempting more writings. I was shocked when the scribbles began to clear up and real words with real meanings began to appear.

Almost all of my writings thus far have been very spiritual, which is actually very humorous to me because I am pretty well known for being outspoken and often irreverent. I am not considered a "stuffy" personality type by any means. I do confess to always feeling very spiritual. Too many instances of odd revelations have occurred in my lifetime to be considered coincidence, and I have a deep and abiding faith in the universal love and guidance of a Higher Power. I do not believe in being Catholic, Baptist, or denominational in any way for myself. I do strongly believe in the pure love of God for mankind.

Purple Mother has given me very few prophetic revelations. Once perhaps, on November 23, 2001, "the boy child is started," and once there was something about an airline catastrophe, and a few other vague references to family that perhaps one could construe as prophetic. She has, however, given me wonderful food for thought. The line I enjoyed most of all is a general favorite by most who have read it, "worry only in prayer, the rest is wasted." How I wish my mother had seen that little wisdom.

One day Purple Mother instructed me to read an entire chapter of Isaiah. I was not happy about that, but I did it. I had never really read or been taught to read a chapter of the Bible in context. In church, usually, only verses were quoted, and only subjects discussed. I must admit that I learned a lot from reading a whole chapter of the Old Testament in context. I also did some research as to the origin of chapters in the Bible. I was surprised.

I do not always trust my writing, and often fear that I subconsciously impose some of my own thoughts into the readings. I consider myself a novice. I do know that the writings have increased my spiritual faith and energy, and I look forward to fullness of spiritual growth in this lifetime and thereafter.

PS from Carolyn: On August 22, Addy was blessed with a "boy child," a grandson born to her youngest son. Evidently Purple Mother knew even before the parents that a "boy child" had been conceived.

On December 8, 2002, while I was writing a very spiritual message on the attributes of God, my spirit writer broke in with: **"BULLETIN: Divine Spirit Cosmos Gives You Beloved New Baby, we tell you the love elevates."** I assumed this message was a confirmation of Addy's *"boy child"* message of November but about a week later my son called to tell me that I would be a great-grandmother. It seems that even before the mothers were aware of their pregnancy, the spirit world knew that babies were forming in their mother's womb. My great-granddaughter was born on August 19, 2002.

About the Author

Carolyn grew up in Washington D.C., where the National Mall was her playground.

After her marriage she moved to Maryland where she taught 8th grade Sunday school in a Methodist Church for several years. During that time, after experiencing a dark night of the soul, she began a personal search for truth that led to automatic writing and a lifetime devoted to spiritual exploration through her writing that led to many spiritual adventures. She has shared her experiences by giving talks and workshops on her book Opening to Fullness of Spirit, reading, facilitating a book study group, focusing on the works of Paul Selig, and taking classes at Unity Church of Charlottesville, where she is an active member.

She is currently an associate editor of *Awareness: exploring spirituality,* an all beliefs inclusive publication dedicated to expanding spiritual paths through professionally written articles and columns.

Other Books By Ozark Mountain Publishing, Inc.

Dolores Cannon
A Soul Remembers Hiroshima
Between Death and Life
Conversations with Nostradamus, Volume I, II, III
The Convoluted Universe -Book One, Two, Three, Four, Five
The Custodians
Five Lives Remembered
Jesus and the Essenes
Keepers of the Garden
Legacy from the Stars
The Legend of Starcrash
The Search for Hidden Sacred Knowledge
They Walked with Jesus
The Three Waves of Volunteers and the New Earth
Aron Abrahamsen
Holiday in Heaven
Out of the Archives – Earth Changes
Justine Alessi & M. E. McMillan
Rebirth of the Oracle
Kathryn/Patrick Andries
Naked In Public
Kathryn Andries
The Big Desire
Dream Doctor
Soul Choices: Six Paths to Find Your Life Purpose
Soul Choices: Six Paths to Fulfilling Relationships
Patrick Andries
Owners Manual for the Mind
Tom Arbino
You Were Destined to be Together
Rev. Keith Bender
The Despiritualized Church
Dan Bird
Waking Up in the Spiritual Age
O.T. Bonnett, M.D./Greg Satre
Reincarnation: The View from Eternity
What I Learned After Medical School
Why Healing Happens
Julia Cannon
Soul Speak – The Language of Your Body
Ronald Chapman
Seeing True
Albert Cheung
The Emperor's Stargate
Jack Churchward
Lifting the Veil on the Lost Continent of Mu
The Stone Tablets of Mu
Sherri Cortland
Guide Group Fridays
Raising Our Vibrations for the New Age
Spiritual Tool Box
Windows of Opportunity
Cinnamon Crow
Chakra Zodiac Healing Oracle
Teen Oracle
Michael Dennis
Morning Coffee with God
God's Many Mansions
Claire Doyle Beland
Luck Doesn't Happen by Chance
Jodi Felice
The Enchanted Garden
Max Flindt/Otto Binder
Mankind: Children of the Stars
Arun & Sunanda Gandhi
The Forgotten Woman
Maiya & Geoff Gray-Cobb
Angels -The Guardians of Your Destiny
Seeds of the Soul
Carolyn Greer Daly
Opening to Fullness of Spirit
Julia Hanson
Awakening To Your Creation
Donald L. Hicks
The Divinity Factor
Anita Holmes
Twidders
Antoinette Lee Howard
Journey Through Fear
Vara Humphreys
The Science of Knowledge
Victoria Hunt
Kiss the Wind
James H. Kent
Past Life Memories As A Confederate Soldier
Mandeep Khera
Why?
Dorothy Leon
Is Jehovah An E.T
Mary Letorney
Discover The Universe Within You
Sture Lönnerstrand
I Have Lived Before
Irene Lucas
Thirty Miracles in Thirty Days
Susan Mack & Natalia Krawetz
My Teachers Wear Fur Coats
Patrick McNamara
Beauty and the Priest
Maureen McGill
Baby It's You
Maureen McGill & Nola Davis
Live From the Other Side
Henry Michaelson
And Jesus Said – A Conversation
Dennis Milner
Kosmos

Other Books By Ozark Mountain Publishing, Inc.

Guy Needler
Avoiding Karma
Beyond the Source – Book 1, Book 2
The History of God
The Origin Speaks
James Nussbaumer
The Master of Everything
Mastering Your own Spiritual Freedom
Sherry O'Brian
Peaks and Valleys
Riet Okken
The Liberating Power of Emotions
John Panella
The Gnostic Papers
Victor Parachin
Sit a Bit
Nikki Pattillo
A Spiritual Evolution
Children of the Stars
Rev. Grant H. Pealer
A Funny Thing Happened on the Way to Heaven
Worlds Beyond Death
Karen Peebles
The Other Side of Suicide
Victoria Pendragon
Born Healers
Feng Shui from the Inside, Out
Sleep Magic
Michael Perlin
Fantastic Adventures in Metaphysics
Walter Pullen
Evolution of the Spirit
Christine Ramos, RN
A Journey Into Being
Debra Rayburn
Let's Get Natural With Herbs
Charmian Redwood
A New Earth Rising
Coming Home to Lemuria
David Rivinus
Always Dreaming
Briceida Ryan
The Ultimate Dictionary of Dream Language
M. Don Schorn
Elder Gods of Antiquity
Legacy of the Elder Gods
Gardens of the Elder Gods
Reincarnation...Stepping Stones of Life
Garnet Schulhauser
Dance of Heavenly Bliss
Dancing Forever with Spirit
Dancing on a Stamp
Annie Stillwater Gray
Education of a Guardian Angel
The Dawn Book
Blair Styra
Don't Change the Channel
Natalie Sudman
Application of Impossible Things
L.R. Sumpter
We Are the Creators
Dee Wallace/Jarrad Hewett
The Big E
Dee Wallace
Conscious Creation
James Wawro
Ask Your Inner Voice
Janie Wells
Embracing the Human Journey
Payment for Passage
Dennis Wheatley/ Maria Wheatley
The Essential Dowsing Guide
Jacquelyn Wiersma
The Zodiac Recipe
Sherry Wilde
The Forgotten Promise
Stuart Wilson & Joanna Prentis
Atlantis and the New Consciousness
Beyond Limitations
The Essenes -Children of the Light
The Magdalene Version
Power of the Magdalene
Robert Winterhalter
The Healing Christ